Willing Wisdom

7 Questions Successful Families Ask

Thomas William Deans, Ph.D.

Published and distributed by
Détente Financial Press Ltd.
PO Box 21123
150 First St.
Orangeville, ON   Canada   L9W 4S7
Tel: (519) 940-4655   Fax: (519) 938-5407
Email: sales@WillingWisdom.com
Contact us for information on author interviews or speaking engagements.

Editor: Donna Dawson, CPE
Cover design: Daphne Robinson
Page composition: Sheila Mahoney

ISBN 978-0-9808910-2-7

Printed in Canada.

To my parents, who set the gold standard caring for my grandparents.

Also by Thomas William Deans, Ph.D.

Every Family's Business:
12 Common Sense Questions to Protect Your Wealth

www.EveryFamilysBusiness.com

Contents

About the Author

Dr. Thomas William Deans is the author of the all-time best-selling family business book, *Every Family's Business: 12 Common Sense Questions to Protect Your Wealth*. He now speaks on the international lecture circuit full time. Having delivered more than 500 speeches, he has built a reputation as a thought leader on the subject of intergenerational wealth transfer.

His lectures and books argue that *family* has emerged as the greatest economic driver of all time. But the question remains: How can wealth be transferred successfully without destroying the recipient and the wealth itself? It is a question for the times, as the greatest generation of wealth creators move toward death in record numbers. Deans explores the idea that communication is crucial to the success of that transfer, and indeed to the success of individuals, families and communities.

Deans starts conversations, but rarely does he finish them, leaving that to readers and their families, friends and trusted advisors.

Willing Wisdom represents a return to the subject of his doctoral research, conducted in the US, Canada and the UK and first published in *Charities and Government* by Manchester University Press.

Tom lives in a forest in the beautiful Hockley Valley in Ontario, Canada, with his wife, two children and four dogs.

Foreword

Many who read the title *Willing Wisdom* will assume that it's another technical estate planning book detailing the intricacies of writing a will or trust agreement. After reading the first page, I knew I was in for something different. *Willing Wisdom* is a book for the ages – written for a generation who has created more surplus wealth than any preceding generation. With this surplus, and perhaps because of it, family dynamics have changed.

For many, planning for the division of assets is a low priority, in part because it has little or no cultural familiarity. But with post war affluence and a bourgeoning middle class, surplus money and its transfer is now something that millions of aging citizens must consider for the first time. For many, what is missing is a common sense approach to transitioning wealth and wisdom to family and charity in a way that deepens relationships and protects wealth.

It's in this context that *Willing Wisdom* offers an optimistic message about what it means to be a successful family. Tom Deans reminds us that success transcends financial wealth and includes preparing our family and community to receive and continue our life's work. The seven questions offered in *Willing Wisdom* give readers a practical approach to holding family meetings and beginning the most important conversations of a lifetime. Add to this the increasing dependency on family to provide late-in-life care, and the issue of financial transparency takes on an unprecedented urgency.

The alternative is family secrets about money – something that seldom builds trust in the relationships that matter most.

If you have been given this book by an advisor, understand that they want the best for you and your family. Most advisors have seen the devastating consequences for families who never share and discuss their estate plans. Advisors, who can help you begin your own family conversations about your will, offer a remarkable gift – the gift of *Willing Wisdom*.

— Grant Robinson FCPA, FCA
Director The SuccessCare Program

Preface

More than 125 million US and Canadian citizens over the age of 18 have no Will. This is a tragedy in the making that will transcend money and is guaranteed to affect relationships profoundly and irreversibly. The time for a new relationship-based approach to estate planning has arrived.

Willing Wisdom seeks to change the perception of what a Will *is* and what it *can* be. It aims to ignite the passion in the hearts and minds of everyday people – people rich and poor – to use their Will to invest in what ought to matter most – relationships. This can happen only through trust and collaboration, as well as trust in collaboration. By talking with intended beneficiaries about death, the potential for living life more fully and purposefully is vastly improved.

This simple idea of making one of the most secretive documents in one's life into a collective work of art will be challenging for many. My hope is that this book will convince you that it's a risk worth taking.

The idea to write *Willing Wisdom* came from watching my mother's parents die. One death – my grandfather's – was comparatively quick. My grandmother's was a long and slow ten-year decline. Despite the significant wealth my grandparents left for family and charity, it is the conversations we shared that I think about the most many years later. In the end, when it came down to their last breaths, only the care provided by my parents, not money or even the promise of money, could purchase the dignified death each experienced.

I'm not sure when I first became curious about why our culture has lost its inquisitiveness about death and dying, but I do know, having delivered my keynote speech on transitioning family wealth to tens of thousands of people around the world, that this trend is worsening. We live in a culture that is in awe of wealth and all that it can provide. We also live in a culture that finds it difficult to talk about and contemplate death. The two are inextricably connected.

Money and control, which often bring comfort in the temporal world, can be lethal and toxic for a generation heading for the exit. As they approach that day, control over money – and healthcare decisions – must often be relinquished. That *more than half the population* will die without a Will, die without any discussion with their family and friends about their end, is symptomatic of a culture entranced and immobilized by the fear of death.

Death phobia is not new. As revealed in Ernest Becker's 1973 Pulitzer Prize–winning book *The Denial of Death* and the work of Irvin Yalom and Stephen Jenkinson, we are a culture afraid of something we can't purchase protection or exemption from – death. But the consequences of not dealing with this fear are far reaching with respect to our ability to live full and extraordinary lives.

Compounding our fear of death is our abiding faith in technology. Many of us have come to believe that we can and must extend life at any price. We speak about death only in the context of extending life, beating a disease, battling to the end, fighting for life, for something that can't be had – living forever.

As long as we are distracted by the idea of extending life at any price, we defer the more interesting and valuable conversation – the one about preparing for death, including writing a Will.

An invitation to your death

This book invites you to invite your family, friends and community to your death *today*, even though your last breath may be many, many years away. Extending that invitation will take both wisdom and courage and you will likely be the first in your lineage to do such a thing.

There can be no better way for us to unlearn our fear of death and dying than to do so in concert with those we love. It's a gift we owe our family, our friends and ourselves. Knowing that we will live on, and that our work will continue, in the hearts of those we love and in our community – our wisdom served faithfully – is an extraordinary lead-up to death.

I hope *Willing Wisdom* can show you why it's important to find your will to Will before the end finds you. Death and dying, just like birth and living, are a collaborative journey monumentally improved when shared with those you love.

Willing Wisdom is as much about protecting and passing on possessions intelligently as it is about passing something more valuable to your beneficiaries – ideals and values. When you artfully build a life for others, it is you who harvests the dividend now and when you are dying. The relationships you leave behind are what shape humanity for all time.

What this book is not

This is not a technical book about the details of writing a Will. Wherever you read the word *Will* in the context of a legal document making provision for the distribution of your assets on death, you can substitute the word with *Trust*. The word *Will* is used to mean merely *one* legal arrangement for the distribution of assets at death. Similarly, *Will* is used in its broadest context to include Guardianship, Financial Power of Attorney, Power of Attorney for Personal Care, Advanced Healthcare Directives and Living Wills. Where it is important to specifically name one of these items to inform the reader more exactingly, an exception is made.

The laws governing Wills and estates vary greatly by jurisdiction and evolve constantly, so I have not dealt with specifics. My hope is that *Willing Wisdom* will be as relevant to readers in fifty years as it is today and as relevant in New York as it is in São Paolo, Sydney, London, Toronto or Beijing.

Lastly, I hope that the seven questions offered in this book give you a new tool to start the most important and personally satisfying exchange of ideas of your life. For it is through conversation – especially about that most awkward subject of all, the transfer of your wealth – that wisdom is revealed and relationships can be deepened.

To begin your own epic journey, sit back and listen in on a conversation that takes place in a Las Vegas lounge between three professional speakers – a psychotherapist, an estate planning lawyer and an intergenerational wealth expert. Their exchange offers a glimpse of the kinds of conversations you might expect to have when you ask your own family, friends and charities of interest those seven questions to discover your will.

After exploring your Will, don't forget to have an estate-planning lawyer draft your Will or update your existing one. Then take the next step: Share it with your beneficiaries. This is how great deaths are conceived and how great families are made to last.

In the end, death is what we make it – so make it familiar by discussing it with the people who matter most in your life.

— *Tom Deans*

Acknowledgments

My first book, *Every Family's Business*, was born from my extraordinary experience working with my father. That book set my course as an author and professional speaker on the subject of business succession planning. My father's gift continues to give and to support the main message of this book: that we leave our children something more valuable than money – wisdom.

From day one of my journey as a speaker, audiences everywhere challenged me to answer one question above all others: How much wealth should we leave family, friends and charities? This book seeks to answer this and many other important questions relating to family, dying and transferring wealth and wisdom.

To the hundreds of advisors and event planners who took a risk and hired a guy with a new message about family businesses, I offer my thanks and gratitude.

The words on these pages were made more precise by the careful hand of my editor, Donna Dawson – thank you for dealing judiciously with my affliction for over-writing.

Special thanks to my wife, Laurie, and two children, Jordan and Nathan, who teach me something new every day – more good fortune for someone who knows he is living a bountiful life.

Lastly, *Willing Wisdom* simply could not have been written without the insight and support of my mother, a prominent and respected psychotherapist. Our daily conversations challenged my assumptions, rounded out my perspective and softened the tone of this book. She reminded me that "soft" family relationship issues are usually the hardest and most complex.

1

The Penny Drops

Close your eyes and take a deep breath.
Now picture your death. Who is holding your hands?

William Cartwright was running late, really late. His flight
into Las Vegas was three hours behind schedule, the lineup at
the taxi stand was longer than usual and, when he finally
scrambled into his cab, the driver, who had to be well over
seventy, drove the speed limit – that was a first. Despite explaining that he was running late to deliver a speech at a convention, William's urging to put the pedal to the metal went
unheeded. As they approached the hotel on the left, William
told the driver it would be quicker if he let William out directly across the street from the hotel.

As the cab rolled to a stop, William tapped the driver on
the shoulder, handed him a $50 bill and told him to keep the
change; he didn't even have time to wait for a receipt. Sliding

out of the cab onto the curb with his small overnight bag, William waited impatiently for the light to change so he could cross the street.

What happened next was like a slow-motion movie. As the walk signal lit up, the sound of screeching tires froze William. In a fleeting second he was staring at the body of a young woman on the other side of the road. She had stepped into the intersection to cross and been struck by a car running the red light. As William made his way across the street, a small crowd gathered around her. She was clearly badly injured. He could hear her moaning in pain, calling for her mother.

William reached for his phone, dialed 911 and pleaded for the operator to send an ambulance. While the operator asked questions, William could see someone holding the injured woman's hand, crying hysterically. The heart-wrenching screams could only be those of a mother.

In what seemed like only seconds, the sound of a siren grew louder. The paramedics arrived at the scene and took control, moving people away from the injured woman. William made his way into the lobby of his hotel. Dazed by what he had just seen, William wondered how on earth he was going to find the focus and energy to deliver his speech.

After quickly checking in, he made his way to the hotel's grand ballroom. The event planner, who looked like she was having a nervous breakdown, was thrilled to see him. She introduced William to the sound man, who wired him up with a lapel microphone, and then led him to the front of the room. While William was being introduced to the audience, he closed his eyes, took a few deep breaths and focused on why he wrote his book and became a professional speaker. The next forty-five minutes were a blur.

"Thank you very much – you've been a terrific audience." The house music seamlessly took over as the applause died down, and William made his way from the stage. He moved quickly to the back of the convention hall to sign copies of his book, hoping to please the event organizer by getting there before any of the 500 attendees could file out of the room without a signed copy.

What had started as a mission to share his experience running and selling his father's business had created the best-selling family business book of all time plus a speaking career that spanned the globe. William loved the adrenaline rush that came with holding a room for an hour with nothing more than ideas, and with the responsibility of shaping and influencing the lives of total strangers.

William loved the book signings too, loved the one-on-one with audience members, and always waited eagerly for "The One." The One was the person who would ask William to sign a book and then proceed to tell him that they disagreed profoundly with his message.

William always knew that he had earned his speaking fee when The One revealed him- or herself. After all, audience members don't bother sharing their dissenting opinions with a speaker who has bored them. William also knew that no one truly remembers a speaker everyone agrees with. Savvy speakers walk a delicate line: being contrarian, persuasive, rational and entertaining without being boorish purely for the sake of being disagreeable.

The One this evening was a woman in her mid-sixties who sheepishly explained that she simply could not wrap her mind around William's message that a family business should never be *gifted* to children but rather *sold* to them, sold to key employees, sold to a competitor – sold to someone, and at the highest possible price.

The woman asked William a straightforward question. "My husband and I started our business more than twenty-five years ago and it's worth about $4 million. Are you suggesting that if our children don't want to *purchase* our business we should sell it and then give them the money when we die?"

William smiled and said, "I'm not suggesting that at all — or even hinting at what you should do with the proceeds from the sale of your business."

"Oh," she replied, "because I was thinking $2 million for each of our kids is a bit much. And then there are their spouses — well, let's just say we've got some issues there."

This wasn't the first time William had been asked this. In fact, the question, "How much should I leave my children?" popped up in virtually every question-and-answer session and every interview William gave. His usual response was informed by his own experience and this evening included a question back to the woman. "Have you spoken to your children about the magnitude of your wealth and what that wealth could be used for when you are no longer alive?"

The woman gasped and jerked her head back in disbelief. "Why would I do that?"

There was something about her indignation that left William both amused and confused, despite witnessing similar responses over the years from people who were considering leaving smaller amounts, like $5,000, to their children.

After he signed her book, William asked the woman for her business card and promised to think about her question and send her a more thoughtful response. Tucking the book into her bag, she smiled awkwardly, knowing the two of them had stumbled into a conversation that was both complex and inappropriate for a public place.

Half an hour later, exhausted and still reeling from the accident he had witnessed, William signed the last book, posed for a photo with the conference host and retreated to his hotel room to freshen up.

As was pretty typical at a convention, William had arranged with two other speakers to meet in the hotel lounge. There was great camaraderie on the speakers' circuit and these post-performance get-togethers were great for decompressing, learning and sharing some laughs.

Both of William's colleagues today were accomplished speakers and best-selling authors. Stephen Walker had three books and more than 1,000 speaking engagements under his belt. A seasoned pro who had taught William a lot about professional speaking, Steve was a lawyer but spent a lot of his time doing media interviews every time someone famous died and left an estate disaster behind. He could tell a lot of stories about the contested estates of people like Michael Jackson, who named his mother but not his father as a beneficiary; both launched legal proceedings. Steve's books and media exposure had made him one of the best-known estate-planning professionals in the country. If you were famous, there was a good chance Stephen Walker had written your Will.

Ashley Norcliff, a psychotherapist, was a powerful speaker with not one, but two books sitting on the *New York Times* best-seller list. She had managed to follow her first book, which had sold more than a million copies in its first six months, with an even more successful book.

It was Ashley's rare combination of intellect and observational skills that had made her a celebrity speaker. But her big break had come when a client, a retired politician, had made public awareness of depression his personal mission and had mentioned her name on *Oprah*. In a follow-up interview, another prominent psychotherapist had described her as intelligent, compassionate and possessing both the integrity and determined curiosity to unearth the deepest mysteries of the human psyche. Her phone hadn't stopped ringing.

It was also well known that Ashley's personal fortune, inherited from her father, a successful industrialist, meant she understood at a deeply personal level what it meant to inherit money and live in the public eye.

William thought about his fellow presenters as he removed his tie and jacket and sank into the plush leather couch in the corner of his suite. He was looking forward to chatting with them. He remembered Steve telling him that more than 125 million adults in the US and Canada had no Will. It was a number so large that William struggled to comprehend the magnitude of the personal devastation that lay waiting. Surely these people love their families – so what is really going on, he wondered?

Glancing at his watch, William realized he had only fifteen minutes to get ready before meeting Steve and Ashley downstairs. He rose from the couch and headed for the shower.

Closing his eyes and tilting his chin down, he let the steaming hot water hit his head and the back of his neck. This always produced a kind of nirvana that moved his mind to a place where ideas flowed and connected randomly. Thinking about some of the stories he had heard on the speaking circuit, William felt something in his gut – a question, a possibility. The misadventures of transferring family wealth were a recurring theme. Maybe, he thought, his family's approach to transferring wealth – something he had watched unfold seamlessly and without fanfare – had led him to completely underappreciate just how many families struggle with this piece of their lives.

Standing perfectly still, William felt, more than heard, the steaming water pound onto the shower floor with a rhythm that enhanced the trance he felt himself drifting into.

It hadn't escaped William's observation that in most of the twenty-five countries in which he had spoken, the culture of money and its effect on families had changed – it had, it seemed, devolved the idea of family, and not evolved it. He remembered Ashley once telling him that of the 2.3 million people who get married in the US and Canada each year, just under half will divorce, leaving about one million people every year experiencing their first major battle over the division of wealth. Was this another example marking our cultural awkwardness with money – a kind of dress rehearsal for the really big fight awaiting family when someone dies without a Will, he wondered?

William turned up the water temperature. As showers went, this one was better than average – lots of water pressure. William thought of the woman he had spoken with at his book signing and wondered why money was impeding her discussions within her family, driving a wedge between the generations rather than bringing them together. The mother of the injured woman stood in such contrast. Why do we wait for a crisis to extend our hand to those we care about – our family, friends and community? he wondered. Why can't we discuss money and share our ideas with the people we love when times are good and death seems so distant and abstract?

Talking about the transfer of money, for most people, seems difficult, William thought, and therefore easier to avoid. Dodging the subject of writing a Will is merely a symptom of giving up on our relationships in the present, he imagined. Whether a frayed relationship is with family, a friend or a whole community, the temptation is too often to avoid a rapprochement or reconciliation. Why give money to a child who expects it? Why give it to a charity that was indifferent to an earlier gift? Why give it to a friend who has a gambling problem? Why bother with any of it, including a Will – when I'm dead, I'm dead – I won't care. I'll let the government deal with my *stuff*.

> No written Will is a symptom of giving-up on relationships

The ringing of the phone snapped him out of his meditation. He didn't need to answer it – he knew exactly who it was and why they were calling. He was late for his meeting with his friends in the lounge. As William shut off the shower he glanced at his watch on the bathroom counter – 7:30. Damn it.

The trip from William's room to the lounge might take longer now that the 500 delegates staying at the hotel knew who he was. There could be delegates on the elevator who would want to chat. William enjoyed these interactions, and on more than one occasion had been invited for dinner or drinks. It was the unplanned and spontaneous post-speech interactions that made his job fun. Often the most innocuous folks turned out to be the most interesting – the ones who shared their stories and taught William further lessons about the dangerous world where family, money and power mixed like a Molotov cocktail.

As he stepped into the empty elevator, his mind drifted again to the woman who had pressed him for help determining how much money she should leave her family in her Will. What is it about Wills, William wondered, that made so many people procrastinate and never get around to writing one? And of those who did, how many left their relatives to discover the full contents of that Will in some austere lawyer's office when they were still grieving? Thinking about whether the young woman hit by the car had survived, William wondered whether the accident would move that family closer together and make the subject of death accessible for everyone to talk about and plan for its inevitability – including writing a Will.

William was finding his audience's response to money and death increasingly baffling. In his family, everyone got thinking and talking early and often about their money and property and its ultimate transfer. Sharing ideas about the transfer of his family's wealth were frequent and varied, not left to the end of someone's life.

The speeding elevator quickly decelerated and stopped at the ground floor. The doors parted, revealing a small crowd of convention delegates pressing forward to enter the elevator – including the woman who had questioned William about the folly of leaving a lot of money to her children. She looked at him and shouted above the din of conversation, "I'm looking forward to continuing our discussion!"

"That makes two of us," replied William.

As the elevator doors closed and the smile of the woman disappeared, William pivoted in the direction of the hotel lounge. He knew his two colleagues would be the perfect people with whom to explore the mystery of why people avoided talking about money, possessions, living and dying – and writing Wills.

2

Ms. Psychotherapy,
Meet Mr. Estate Planning

Close your eyes and take a deep breath. Now ask yourself...
What will I really be remembered for?

William headed straight to the lounge. It was a short walk through the lobby and down a hallway hung with six ornate chandeliers. As he passed through the double doors into the dimly lit lounge he could see that it was large – typical of Las Vegas, where everything was super-sized. It was a beautiful room, even by Vegas standards, with low rich leather chairs and couches, warm earth-tone carpeting and exceptional art on the walls. Potted palms arched over conversation areas. The piano in the back corner created the perfect casual but elegant mood. As William entered, he spotted his colleagues to the right of the piano and motioned to the hostess in their direction. She smiled and gestured for him to proceed.

As he approached the table where Ashley and Steve were sitting, Ashley waved and called out, "We were just about to send out a search party!"

William took a seat facing the piano. "Sorry I'm late, guys. I've had a heck of a day – delayed flight, the slowest taxi driver on the planet and to top it all off I witnessed an awful accident – a woman struck by a car right outside the hotel just as I arrived. I'm not even sure she survived. I have to say, I can't even remember giving my speech."

"How awful," replied Ashley. "I'm so sorry to hear that. You alright?"

"I'll be fine, thanks," replied William, "but it sure hits home."

"That's bad," agreed Steve. "I remember in New York once I was about to step off the curb and a total stranger grabbed my arm and yanked me back as a taxi flew past. The line between life and death is shockingly thin. I think we've all had close calls and then sat back and said, 'I wonder why my number didn't come up?'"

"This thing called life is bizarre," concurred William, resigning himself to what he'd experienced. Wanting to change the subject, he added, "Plus my book signing went longer than usual."

"So you sold all five copies?" Steve said brightly, trying to lighten the mood.

"Ha ha. Who writes your material?" William shot back. "Truth is," he continued, "I got into a bit of a discussion with a woman wanting to know how much money she should leave her children in her Will. I think she really believed I had a magic number, a percentage or a formula I could give her."

Steve ran his hands through his hair. "Tell me you didn't give her a number."

"Absolutely not. But I did do a Socratic maneuver and answered her question with a question. I asked whether she had told her kids that she and her husband were worth at least $4 million."

"Four mill... she wasn't the one wearing a red dress, six rows from the front on the left, was she?"

"Ah yeah, Steve, you know I'm sitting here right," said Ashley.

Ignoring the exchange, William continued. "You wouldn't believe her response."

Steve smirked and said, "William, I'm an estate planning attorney. There's nothing you can tell me about people and money I haven't heard a thousand times."

"Well, she as much as laughed at me and said, 'why would I tell my children how much money I have?' But tell me, Steve. You're the estate planner to the stars. How many of your clients *do* tell their children about the full extent of their assets while they're still alive and thinking clearly?"

Steve, who had shifted his attention to the drinks menu, peered over the top of his reading glasses and responded, "You're joking, right?"

"No. Seriously, what percentage?"

Steve rolled out his bottom lip, cocked his head and looked up into space in search of his answer. "I'd say less than ten percent."

"Are you telling me that ninety percent of your clients' children will find out the full extent of their parents' wealth and wisdom *after* they're dead – like at the reading of the Will in your office?"

"Yep. Any lawyer can tell you stories of clients learning for the first time the contents of a Will and going ballistic. Some lawyers deliberately hold these meetings at night or early in the morning so that other clients in the office don't hear the drama unfolding. The biggest meltdowns always come from people who had been told they were going to receive something and then find out they received nothing. But the crème de la crème is when a Will has been redrafted late in someone's life, with the whole family disinherited completely and a much younger, ahem, 'caregiver' made sole beneficiary. Those are fun. And remember, that's ten percent of the people who actually *have* Wills. The better question is, how many people even really speak to their children honestly about their wealth at all?"

"And…?" William waited. "The answer is…?"

"Easy," Steve answered, tossing down the drinks menu. "One."

"One percent?" asked Ashley, incredulous.

"No, one person! Mother Teresa – and she had no wealth and no kids."

Steve continued as Ashley and William laughed. "Look, you need to understand. People, money, emotions, dying – it's the perfect combo for some great drama. I like to remind my audiences that those reading-of-the-Will meetings are like Baskin Robbins: they come in at least thirty-one flavors. Just when you think you've seen it all, a new flavor is invented, some new dynamic emerges and you sit back and say 'wow, that is pure craziness.' If you have an hour or ten, I could tell you about some family meetings that still make me jackknife awake at night in terror. And I swear, every relative, friend or charity cut out of a person's Will thinks *I* was behind the plot. I have a recurring nightmare where I'm stuck in an elevator with this insane woman who is trying to mess me up."

Ashley leaned forward, eyes wide, dead serious. "Steve, could it be that the woman in the elevator isn't really after you, but rather that your dream is a metaphor? Perhaps the woman in your dream is your mother and instead you're afraid she might leave? Sounds like you might have a touch of LSA."

"What the heck is that?" asked Steve with some urgency.

"Lingering separation anxiety," she said. "You might find regression therapy helpful. I'd be happy to refer you to a colleague in New York if you'd like."

Steve wasn't sure if Ashley was being serious or stringing him along, but didn't want to acknowledge that she might be on to something. So he said, "I'll go into therapy if William goes too. That'll teach me to tell a dream to a psychotherapist."

Before Ashley could respond, William piped up, "I had a dream that you —" giving Steve the double-handed point "— bought the first round of drinks."

Hearing the laughter and seeing Steve look up, the waiter approached. "Looks like the party has started, so can I get you some drinks?"

"Club soda and lime, please," said Ashley.

"I'll have a Diet Coke," Steve said. "I need to watch my girlish figure." Turning to William, he said, "I went to button my jacket today with one hand when I was on stage and let's just say it turned into a very public two-handed maneuver."

The waiter turned to William. "I'll have a piña colada, please."

"Thank you," said the waiter, spinning on his heel.

The waiter was no sooner out of earshot than Steve remarked, "Seriously? A piña colada? You do know we're in Las Vegas and not Barbados, right?"

William ignored Steve and turned to Ashley. "In your professional opinion as an accomplished psychotherapist, do you think Steve's recurring bedwetting explains why he avoids the emotional needs of his clients and treats the whole subject of Wills and estate planning as a technical issue, or is it the other way around? I mean really, what comes first?"

Steve smirked, "Oh, that's a low blow."

"But seriously," William said, "what is it with lawyers and Wills? For the last couple of years now I've been asking my audiences how many people have Wills and I'm getting something like half the people putting up their hands. When I ask how many people have updated their Wills in the past five years, I lose another half of the hands. This tells me that in my typical audience — and these are mostly people who *own businesses*, remember – I only have something like twenty-five percent who have given some serious thought to leaving their family, friends and community with something other than total chaos.

"You know, guys," William confessed, "that lady today that I told you about kind of shook me up. I mean, I've been traveling around the world for five years doing all sorts of interviews and speeches, saying never *give* your business to your children. If they don't want to *buy* the business, then sell it and give your wealth instead. I've come to understand that the majority of people, even if they do heed my advice, will die without a Will and without ever having discussed with their kids what they will inherit and what the money can and should be used to accomplish today and in the future."

"You, sir," replied Steve, face serious, "are an idiot. Do you have any idea what kids with money do when their parents die? They come here" – gesturing toward the picture window overlooking the Strip – "they come to Sin City in droves and they blow it as fast as they were given it. And do you have any idea what charities can do with significant gifts when they're given without thoughtful direction?"

Ashley spoke. "William, it strikes me that there are two issues here. One, why don't people write Wills, and two, why don't they write proper, thoughtful, insightful and intelligent Wills and share them with their intended beneficiaries before they die? I can tell you," she continued, wanting to answer her own questions, "that avoidance and fear of anything relating to death can paralyze people, paralyze their thinking and prevent them from acting on some of life's most important issues."

"So," interjected William, "the lady who confronted me today is likely going to procrastinate indefinitely, year after year, and avoid a meaningful conversation with her intended beneficiaries about the contents of her Will because she is afraid of dying?"

Ashley responded, "It's not really procrastination. It's something much deeper that operates at the subconscious level that makes the act of planning for one's death – like writing a Will – an inherently fearful exercise. I had one client who was diagnosed with terminal cancer and given three months to live. Even after being told to get her affairs in order, she ignored everything and died without a Will. The ensuing legal battle between her children over her sizable estate was awful – it tore the family apart and I presume that only the lawyers got rich."

"Hey, we have to feed our families too!" Steve said. He took the opportunity to give his take on the matter. "For some people, though, I think a Will is simply another expense to be avoided, like 'a Will is for the benefit of my family – if I'm not here, how does it benefit me? Besides, the car needs new tires. Next year,' they say, and next year comes and next year goes. I hear it all the time: 'I'm busy, but I'll get to it,' or 'I keep forgetting!'"

William nodded. "I've had people in my audiences say, 'why pay for a Will when the government will simply divide up my stuff and give it to the same people I'd give it to anyway?'"

Ashley continued, shaking her head. "To this day I wonder what prevented my client from writing her Will. All I can tell you is that procrastination is a handy and simple explanation but that's not it, at least not in this case. It was something so much more complex. She had time – but not much, she knew the implications of not writing a Will, she had the resources to get one done and yet she never did. The only clue she gave me was an off-the-cuff comment during one of our sessions that she would probably die as soon as the ink was dry on her Will. It was as if she felt that expressing her will to pass on her worldly possessions would rob her of something today and expedite her death. In a way, the preparation of a Will is the preparation of the mind for the inevitable – one's will, and by that I mean one's spirit, is a delicate concept informed by experience, by superstition but mostly by the fear of the darkness that many presume awaits us."

"Well, that's a cheery assessment," concluded Steve. "Hopefully the guy playing the piano doesn't know any Leonard Cohen songs or we'll all be slitting our wrists."

William sat in silence for a moment. Turning to Steve, he said, "So how much of what Ashley just said rings true to you? Is this the kind of stuff you see in your estate planning practice?"

"Without question. Except we are a profession that takes instruction." Adopting a somewhat sarcastic tone, he continued, "It's not our place to put the client on the couch and say, 'before we draft your Will I want to show you a couple of ink blots and I want you to tell me where you see your money going.' We'll generally ask a couple of open-ended questions to get a basic feel for their plan. There is big danger in guiding clients too forcefully – danger in being too prescriptive about how they should divide their assets. I can tell you in my early days I was beaten up badly when I pushed my agenda on my clients and projected my own ideas on what should be in their Will."

Leaning forward in his chair and dropping his voice, Steve continued. "This isn't for public consumption, but in my first year of practice a client's son sued me for professional misconduct, claiming I had planted the idea in his father's mind that the kid should be disinherited. That he had a drug problem, couldn't hold a job and had had more than a couple of brushes with the law probably helped me dodge that bullet. But it was a valuable lesson. From that day forward I promised myself I would *draft* a client's Will but never again *write* one. I promised myself to avoid what I think you folks in the touchy-feely world call *transference*."

"Oh, that *is* impressive," remarked Ashley.

"So really what you're saying –" William questioned, "and don't get me wrong, I'm not being critical of the legal profession – is that a client is largely on their own when it comes to deciding who'll get what – who'll get the car, the cottage, the cash, the business, the furniture, the insurance, hell, even the cat?"

"All – on – their – own," replied Steve.

Just then the waiter reached them with their drinks on a tray that he whipped around like a circus performer. "Here you go, ma'am," placing the club soda in front of Ashley, "and for you, sir," passing Steve his drink. William's piña colada, sporting a lime-green umbrella and a skewer of fruit, stood tall in the center of the tray. The waiter lowered the tray dramatically and presented the drink to William. "And for you."

"William, dude, what are you, like, six years old?" guffawed Steve as the waiter turned.

William simply smiled. He leaned back in his chair with his cocktail and pulled a piece of pineapple off the skewer with his teeth. After a pause he said, "So how do we help these people? Maybe one of us should write a book."

"Sure, in my spare time," said Steve.

"I'm done with writing books," said Ashley.

The three sat in silence, sipping their drinks, the piano playing quietly. Then William sat up. "I think the key to solving this monumental problem could lie with advisors – they're pivotal to the kind and magnitude of change we need. By advisor I mean not just lawyers, I mean wealth advisors, insurance professionals, accountants, doctors, spiritual leaders and yes, even psychotherapists. These trusted counselors are in a privileged position to open a dialog with clients and their beneficiaries to get the most important legal document in someone's life put in place.

"We have to keep in mind that the Will isn't just a document about setting up trusts and reviewing tax liabilities," he continued, "nor is it just a document that helps us think about selecting the right kind of investment and insurance strategies. It's so much more. It's a document for framing an intelligent discussion about *how* and *what* we leave our family, friends and community. I believe it transcends money and possessions. I'm thinking out loud here, but I truly believe that a Will is the single greatest entry point for every one of these advisors to go further with their planning to serve their clients and themselves by protecting clients from the biggest threat of all."

"Which is?" asked Ashley.

"Their own fear of death," responded William. "Too many people hijack their own legacies, failing themselves first and their family next because of an unrelenting fear about the lead-up to death and the dependence on others for care.

"When we hear at funerals that someone will live on in the hearts of the people who cared about him, I think a lot of people don't realize that 'living on' doesn't just happen. How we are remembered and how *much* we are remembered is a reflection of how much our life has been about ourselves and how much it has been about others we have touched through our ideas, words and actions."

William leaned forward, his thoughts coming together. "The fear of death is proportional, isn't it, to how much our life has been about acquiring wealth to purchase more stuff versus using wealth to build great relationships. Do you see the difference? It's subtle – money, that thing that too often divides, is one thing that can build relationships. But it takes time and wisdom informed through conversation – there is no shortcut. And therein lies the challenge – *talking* about money and ideas.

"I can appreciate that advisors feel they can only push and prod on this subject so far. I can tell you that my own financial advisor was totally devastated when a long-time client died intestate – died without a Will."

"Ah, yeah, I know what intestate means," laughed Steve.

"He told me some of the story," continued William. "I could see that he took it hard, took it as a failure on his part to serve his client and the client's family. It was as if he hadn't had the courage to push hard enough, long enough or often enough to get proof that the bloody Will was actually written and signed."

William paused for a sip. "He said that in the future he would threaten to quit advising a client if they flat out resisted drafting their Will over a specified period of time. I don't know whether he's ever had to part ways with a client since making that proclamation, but I do know he has personally made appointments for clients who didn't have a lawyer or a Will and has even gone so far as to pick them up at their house and drive them to those appointments to get it done. He sends clients a reminder every year to review their Wills – I know because I receive that letter every year as my birthday approaches."

"Can you give me his card?" asked Ashley. "I could use an advisor like that!"

"Absolutely. But really – don't you think that at the end of the day a Will is simply the most important estate planning document there is? It's the document that takes someone's entire life's work and divides it into the hands of others. Tragically, it's been positioned as a private and solitary document, where more secrecy somehow equals a better plan."

"But isn't that what we do," asked Steve, "keep our financial affairs secret, always refusing to discuss what our resources can accomplish?"

"Frankly," replied William, "I think the way our culture approaches Wills is flawed. The way most people handle it, it's a depressing, oppressive document that misleads people and their families into believing that the essence of a Will is secrecy. I'm coming to see that it's precisely this secrecy that's tearing people, families and communities apart. When born from silence, a Will leaves little but questions, acrimony, regret, depression, shame, loss, vitriol, confusion… shall I go on? A Will, we are led to believe, is an *end-of-life* document. And I have to tell you guys I believe that nothing could be farther from the truth. I've given this some thought now – maybe I *could* write a book that advances two straightforward and simple ideas."

"Only two?" interjected Steve.

"Yeah, but they're big ideas. First, that a Will should be one of the most exciting documents we write, not isolated from our beneficiaries but rather *in collaboration* with them. I believe it's the collaboration between the people and organizations we intend to share our wealth with that informs our giving decisions in both directions. And by this I mean that those considering their Will are teaching family, friends and charitable organizations about how their wealth was acquired and the responsibilities that go with inheriting that wealth."

A Will should be the most exciting document you write

"Seems straightforward enough," agreed Ashley.

"In return," continued William, "I see intended beneficiaries teaching those doing the giving about how they might deploy gifts in a new and changing world. Reciprocity – a reciprocal Will, if you will. I think part of what makes dying so final and depressing for many is the idea that nothing you did over the course of your life continues after you're dead. We have given up on the idea that the best of what we can offer of ourselves, our experience, will weave itself forward through time with those to whom we have imparted our wisdom. Passing ideas fueled by money to make something better for humanity – who's talking about that?"

"That's a rather optimistic view of humanity's potential," chuckled Steve.

"I know it is. But why does every generation need to reinvent the wheel – the process of willing – often repeating mistakes or, more tragically, missing the incredible opportunity to share the great life lessons learned with the view of building enduring families? But this is what happens when someone writing a Will has never participated in a Will-making process because their parents kept the whole thing secret. Think about it. We teach our kids how to play sports, how to read; we teach them about life, but have forgotten about preparing them for death."

"As I think about it," said Ashley, "in a world where everyone is living longer, it's now reasonable to expect to have four generations alive at one time – great-grandparents, grandparents, parents and children. What an amazing opportunity for each generation to guide and inform the other in both directions about their Wills."

"Exactly," replied William, excited that Ashley could see the urgency of his message. "Secret Wills? Secret family wishes? I think the outcome is as certain as hurricane season in the Caribbean. I don't understand it! A Will is an amazing opportunity for family to engage in an open conversation about ideas that provide both continuity and exciting change in a family. Even for those without children, doesn't a Will afford the person doing the giving an extraordinary opportunity to talk to nieces, nephews, friends and charities and share their dreams for the future?

"Isn't this what a Will should be," William continued, on a roll, "a document that inspires conversation and creativity, with the past informing and shaping the future? Why have we let the taxman hijack our Wills by reducing them to an estate planning document that aims to save tax, full stop? No wonder people don't write Wills. It hasn't really been branded as a very sexy topic, has it? Death and taxes – now there's an awesome one-two punch. Little wonder only half of all people have a Will."

"Maybe you *should* write a book," said Steve. "I'm sensing something touchy-feely."

"Hey, call it what you want," responded William, but the idea of a book was growing on him. "All I know is that what's been tried isn't working – fewer and fewer people are writing Wills and it's destroying families. Talking about money is the last taboo – we are culturally programmed to avoid it. In ancient times, when families sat around campfires telling stories about elders who had died, the legacies being transferred weren't physical possessions, but rather something far more valuable and enduring. There was no need for Wills – the piece of paper. The only gift passed forward was a person's will – their spirit. There were no secrets, no jealousy about who got what. The only asset of value was the knowledge given every day with equanimity to everyone sitting around that fire with the capacity and interest to listen and learn through discussion. If you were smart you listened, learned and acted. It didn't matter if you were the first-born or the fifth-born or indeed whether you were family at all. In the end it was only knowledge that people had to give. Isn't this precisely what we have lost?"

"Uh-oh, I sense a man on a mission," Steve called out.

Ashley ignored him. "I suppose it *is* something that has slipped out of much of our collective culture."

"Precisely," William agreed. "The distant past stands in such contrast to modern times, when we invest so much of our hope for the future in the stuff we have accumulated during our life, in our money, in wealth, that we have utterly forgotten to talk to and teach our children about our will to change the world first through our actions and ultimately through our progeny, our friends and our community when we are dead.

"Is a life well-lived really measured by how much wealth we acquire or is it measured instead by the condition in which we leave our relationships? Do we leave those who matter in our lives fighting over our stuff or are we capable of something better, something more inspiring? Have we really lost faith in those we are closest to to be more than we are, more in every sense of the word, including having more and doing more in our name and in our memory? Have we lost touch with what *legacy* and *humanity* mean? I think we need to revive the old abandoned idea that celebrated the tradition of wise counsel."

He paused for a drink. "But how do we convince a generation nearing the end of their lives to reassert their control over their own clock and inspire them to lead conversations that could educate and guide their family, their friends and the charities they support

Will you leave people fighting over your stuff?

through their own struggles with money and what money can and can't accomplish? Could that not be their ultimate enduring gift to their beneficiaries – dialog, wisdom and then, and only then, perhaps the gift of some money?"

"You do have a dream," Ashley said. "No one can accuse you of thinking small!"

"Well, not so fast, Willy my boy," interjected Steve. "That was a compelling speech but stop and think about where you're going with this. First, if you think you can tell people how much of their money they should leave to whom, prepare yourself to get knocked down a peg or two. It can't be done. Frankly, you're insane for thinking you can. Of the 5,000 or so Wills I've drafted for clients, not very many were the same. And second, if you think people are going to sit down with their beneficiaries and share the contents of their Will – no wait, what did you say? Sit down and 'collaborate' on their Will with their beneficiaries, you're dreaming. Naive doesn't begin to describe the direction you're heading."

"So we should leave the whole subject alone and continue to watch half of all people die without a Will and then leave it to the government to divide up their life savings, giving it to people they may not have wanted to get their money and tax it like crazy, leaving wrecked families in its wake?" William asked. "Why? Just because that's the way it's always been done? I think that's a huge cop-out."

"Here, here," said Ashley.

William continued, "I'm not suggesting that every Will should be the same, but the *process* a family adopts to write Wills can be the same. The secret lies in the questions they ask, not the answers. In my own family, there are a number of questions we ask each other every year at our family meeting, and these drive conversation about our money and how it will eventually transfer. I can't tell you how many times I've been through these questions. They've become so routine they seem obvious. Other people could do the same thing."

"Did you say *family meeting?*" asked Steve. "Well heads up again, William – not everyone has family meetings. The last thing most of my clients would want to do is put everyone in a room and talk about their money. And I have seen very few people sit down and engage in a thoughtful discussion with their favorite charities about what their money can accomplish. Most charities receive money without any strings attached – no direction, no prior discussion, no imagination, just cold hard cash. There's a better chance of peace in the world than of people starting to seriously engage their beneficiaries in a dialog in the preparation of their Will. People just aren't gonna do it."

"Look, Steve," William said, "you know and I know that there is no joy in knowing you haven't addressed a problem. It sits there in the back of your mind, eating away at your sense of self, preventing you from experiencing real happiness because you've lacked the courage to dive in and do your own hard work. The unresolved business shapes and taints relationships. Sadly, it's our equivocation about our death that leads to equivocation about our life."

"That's an interesting way of putting it," said Ashley, pulling a notepad from her bag and jotting down a note.

William continued. "What I'm imagining is an approach to writing a Will that's more akin to giving the perfect birthday gift. You know that feeling you get when you've thought long and hard about a gift, you've expended effort, you've invested time and creativity, and you go out and search for it – you either buy it or make it yourself – you wrap it perfectly and then you have to wait to give it? And the waiting's so difficult because you're so darn excited about this gift because it's perfect and it says 'I *know* you, I know what you like, what you want, what you need – what will make you happy.' The act of giving is *informed*. I can't tell you how many times my wife has given me a gift weeks before my birthday. Why can't we muster the same excitement when it comes to the biggest gift of them all – our entire life's work, our entire life's savings, everything? Why is our last Will so morose and sad, not the exciting celebration it ought to be?"

"Well, the quick answer," offered Steve, "is that when you're dead, you're not actually at the party. And let me get this straight: Did you say you think asking some *questions* will actually make people enthusiastic about writing their Will? Man, I don't know what you ate for breakfast today, but I'm guessing someone put dream berries in your cereal. A Will is something people do. It's like cleaning out the garage – an unpleasant chore to strike off the to-do list. Maybe that book's not such a great idea after all. You're heading into dangerous waters and besides, you're not even a lawyer."

"But that," said Ashley, "is exactly why such a book could work. This isn't about writing Wills, it's about peoples' *will* – about all our struggles and our inability to deal with death and dying and about leaving something profound in this world that survives."

Steve leaned forward and fixed his gaze on William. "Look, don't get me wrong, buddy, there's nothing I'd like more than to be able to give my clients a list of questions and say 'please answer these before we meet next week so that I can draft your

Will in such a way that it will put my entire litigation team out of business.' I'm just saying, don't get your hopes up."

Ashley said, "I still think you're missing the point, Steve. I can see how this idea could have great therapeutic value and make a great contribution to a lot of families. I don't think there's anything out there that offers individuals a simple tool to reconnect with themselves, their family and their community. And to do it by focusing on *money* – precisely the one thing that usually pulls people and relationships apart – it's sheer genius."

Lightening the mood, Ashley added, "And if William does write a book, kids who have healthy relationships with their parents will buy it, hand out lots of copies to family members and get cracking with their family meetings. They know the clock is ticking and the taxman is waiting. What a great conversation starter."

"Or a ticking time bomb," said Steve. "I'm still not convinced that families are ready to release their fear of dying and begin discussing transferring their money and wisdom. Then again," he added, draining his glass, "the only real loser in a mass rethink would be the government."

"Oh absolutely," agreed Ashley. "You're going to be a huge hit with the taxman, William. Best brace yourself for an audit because if you get everyone *willing*, we're talking about millions, maybe billions, of dollars of tax revenue that governments won't be collecting."

Steve chimed in, "Oh, it's billions, all right. I attended an international convention of estate planners last year in Monaco and that same number, fifty percent, kept popping up from every country in attendance, from the UK to Brazil to Australia to South Africa. People there aren't writing Wills either. So what I'm thinking is that William here won't just be on America's most wanted list, he'll be wanted by every government that has to introduce new taxes to replace the lost revenue thanks to his Will to Will Campaign."

"It *is* a campaign – a public awareness campaign!" agreed William.

"One more thing," Steve continued. "Don't be thinking that the only people who don't write Wills are uneducated or poor. Billionaires and geniuses are as apt to mangle their estate planning as anyone else. More stuff and more wealth usually spells more trouble, actually. The lack of will – in both senses of the word – cuts across every income level, class, race, culture, religion and country on this planet."

"That's kind of surprising," responded William. "I mean, if you're a millionaire surely you have access to great advice, great advisors, great plans."

"Yes indeed," agreed Steve. "And when those great advisors prepare a great plan and draft a brilliant Will and a Trust agreement but the papers remain unsigned, that and $1.75 will get you a cup of coffee. And let me be clear: When I say that you can't generalize about what kind of person doesn't write a Will, let me illustrate. Did you know that not one, not two, but *four* US presidents died without a Will? And here's the best part: Two of them were lawyers."

"You've got to be kidding. Which two?" asked William.

"Andrew Johnston and Abraham Lincoln. Now you'd be hard pressed to find two more highly accomplished men, both with plenty of will to lead their country, but apparently not enough will to lead their own family."

Ashley finished her drink. "Yes – maybe they exercised all their will for their country and had nothing left for their family. Then again, maybe legions of people simply don't give a damn about their families. Maybe that's the simple, honest truth about why they don't write a Will. Maybe it's the same reason people don't buy life insurance: 'When I'm dead there's nothing in it for me, so forget it.' And you can see that if a family doesn't know how to explore their past – what they've done well with money and where they've fallen short – they'll be destined to repeat it."

"Ouch," said Steve. "That's a brutal assessment, especially coming from a psychotherapist. I mean, aren't you in the group-hug business?" Ashley's left eyebrow rose sharply and her direct gaze froze Steve for a moment before he continued hastily. "But you're right. And something that most people don't think about is that when someone dies without a Will, and their estate is relegated to probate court, it's a public forum for the whole world to take a peek and pass judgment on how much or little was accumulated and about how the deceased apparently had no interest in giving to specific people or organizations with thought and care."

Ashley said, "As shocking as it may seem, I have to admit that Steve is right, in one respect, anyway. In advocating for this kind of change you're going to be pushing some buttons. Not everyone will be happy with your message."

"Last time I checked the history books," William interjected, "anyone who pushed for positive change and did a good job didn't start by asking, 'how can I make everyone happy?'"

"Brave words," said Steve, "but tell me: You said you and your family sit down every year at family meetings and ask a series of questions about money, about who should get what, when and how. What are those questions?"

"I thought you'd never ask. But before I get there I need to ask you a question or two."

3

The Cake Tastes
Sweeter on Your Willday

Close your eyes and take a deep breath.
Now recall the first name of even one of your
great-great-grandmothers.

The piano player had done a remarkable job of offering music from at least five decades, as if he had scanned the crowd and noted the different generations in the room and delivered something for everyone. In a way, the piano player was showing his awareness of generational differences, William reflected.

William surveyed the room for a few moments. His intuition told him that the guy behind the piano playing a number of Billy Joel songs almost surely meant that earlier the waitress he was watching had declared herself a fan of the eighties pop star. This piano man was working it.

Aren't we all working it, William thought. Aren't we all working on something shyly, playing at life, casting around for clues about why we are here. Despite William's brave words about a new way to encourage people to write Wills, he wondered why he had this need to tackle the hard emotional subjects with audiences around the world.

Writing a book on Wills would be the easy part. There is time and space between writer and reader. It was the specter of taking his message about Wills on the road – the thought of standing on stage and inspiring the confused and the fearful as they wrestled with money and their own mortality – that moved William to press for more thoughts from his two colleagues.

Steve the technician and devil's advocate, offering reality checks and concrete answers about money in the here and now, and Ashley the psychotherapist, offering the simple adage that only the examined life is worth living. Her thinking wasn't about offering anyone clues on how to live the perfect life, rather simply how to be good enough *at life*. William knew Ashley's perspective had value, especially when it came to answering the question of why people don't write Wills and why, when they do, they write them in secret without sharing with their beneficiaries.

For some people, the exercise of writing a Will is all business, done quickly, efficiently, in isolation, and to the letter of the law – a purely technical process. For others, the act of willing is about instinct, reflection and self-preservation – something done, again, in isolation, where the laws of human nature reign over the laws applied in litigation.

It was at the extremes of both worlds where the act of willing was falling short of producing anything of real consequence. For both failed to acknowledge that death can be a collaboration and that the best death is one we see coming, one whose certainty is absolute and if shared with the people we entrust to continue our work, a death well lived.

For the living, isn't a Will the perfect place to start sharing ideas with the people we love and trust while we're all healthy and thinking clearly? Isn't a Will the perfect place to talk about how we can end our life story with an exclamation mark, not a question mark?

William knew that dying with *nothing* meant dying with *everything*. He had witnessed the deaths of his grandparents, he had seen the withering, had seen how extraordinarily ordinary, almost routine, their death was. These deaths were so utterly indifferent to the significant wealth of the dying that death seemed to mock the very pursuit of wealth. Wealth had no currency in matters of the heart, where the real dying was taking place. For at that very last moment, when time stands still, when the last breath is released, we are all strikingly equal and ordinary. Surely that last breath is precipitated with greater ease and purpose when we have released our grip on our stuff and arranged for its use by others in a world we no longer play in. Conversely, imagine someone who in that final moment of lucidity knows the certainty of their fate, knows they have made no arrangements for the disposition of their possessions, and then changes their mind, wishing they had, but now cannot exercise their will. Does this explain the terror and wretchedness on the faces of so many who die?

"William, what were you thinking?" Steve waited, and he and Ashley looked expectantly at William. "Are you still with us, buddy?"

"What? Yeah, sorry. What?"

"Where were you?" asked Ashley, laughing.

"I was thinking about the possibility of that book about Wills. I'm absolutely certain there's a need. I've spoken to thousands of people since the release of my first book, and just like that woman today, so many are struggling to find and express their will. Eyes never lie. I've looked into too many from my side of the podium to know that we need a new approach when it comes to connecting family, friends and community to their own wealth and wisdom. My encounter with that lady at my book signing, and seeing that woman lying on the pavement holding her mother's hand, was the tipping point. I can't keep giving speeches about selling the family business and passing on wealth when I've got this big question mark in my mind about the dangers of people leaving lots of money to family without any *context* about how it can and should be deployed or even worse, leaving a heck of a mess behind when they die without a Will."

William looked at Steve and Ashley to see if they were still interested in the topic. He was beginning to feel he might be pushing it. "No offence, Steve, but I don't think the world needs another technical book on how to write a Will, but rather something that gives the reader a roadmap, a *process* to follow to find their will to write their Will. That half of all people die without one probably means it's time for a new approach, don't you think?"

Sitting back in his chair, William continued. "I'm not talking about inventing a new $10 do-it-yourself Will kit. What I'm proposing is something very different. I want to help people understand their will – their ability to shape their world today and long after they die. I think most people don't have a clue how to start a conversation with their family or anyone else about how they will transfer assets when they die. Silence becomes the norm, not just for one generation but for succeeding generations because they know nothing else – because they're taught nothing else. Silence is the great destroyer of wealth, relationships and human potential.

"Beneficiaries," William continued, lifting his empty glass and setting it down again, "or at least those who *think* they'll inherit something, can't raise the subject because they think they'll look like they're pushing an agenda, that they have their hands out. And those who should be doing the planning don't want to raise the subject because it feels like opening a can of worms. It's easier to let sleeping dogs lie. And so what do we get? Nothing. And that's the plan for half of the 350 million Americans and Canadians alive today, who tiptoe around the subject of death and the transfer of wealth as if the problem doesn't exit, can't exist, if we simply give it a wide berth.

"This could be a book not so much about Wills as about preparation for death. There is so much dancing around the subject of death that we hardly recognize it when we hear it. I remember buying life insurance from one professional who called it what it was – death insurance. I loved his honesty, and so I bought into his thoughtful plan to provide for my family in the event that I no longer could."

Steve nodded. "I couldn't agree more. We do need to change the discourse about the most obvious event in life – death."

William added, "The only problem is we don't know when the clock will stop. So shouldn't we start with the end in mind *today*? We need to get people to get together and talk about death and the disposition of their assets and wisdom now, and celebrate it."

Catching up, Steve said, "Okay, I see where this is going. It would be one of those sessions where the person with all the money, the person writing the Will, is going to gather all their potential beneficiaries and grill them, and the one with the best answers gets the lion's share of the estate – whip them into shape and get them focused and competing for the prize."

William quickly shook his head. "Not at all. That's not how it feels when my parents discuss their Wills. We've always had these discussions on our birthdays, and my parents have always claimed that talking about their Will on that day was a gift to themselves. My mother has said it makes perfect sense that we talk about who will continue her life's work when she has died, on the very day marking her entry into the world. Steve, talking about death in our family is an Olympic sport – except we don't wait four years between updates. We train for our death every day. We know that to go forward as individuals we need to converse as a family – looking back in time together."

Ashley raised her hand slightly to interrupt, but then paused. She pursed her lips and looked at William. "Ah, William. I think I need to point out that how your family handles this is not entirely... typical. You know? Most people don't chat about their own deaths on their birthday. People just don't do that."

Fidgeting, William pushed his empty glass toward the center of the table. "Well, we do. My mother always believed that her birthday should be called her willday. It is, after all, her special day, when her will is honored and celebrated, the day we've served her favorite meal and offered her gifts. Gifts! We've always offered gifts on the day we speak about dying."

William noticed that Steve and Ashley were looking at him a bit blankly. "It's not weird or anything, honestly. Let me back up a bit and tell you how it works."

"I was eighteen when I signed my first Will – at the time, I thought it was an odd birthday present from my parents, who had arranged it. They explained that as an adult you not only begin to take care of yourself, but also of those you love. It's a turning point, an evolution. As adults, we ought to shift our consciousness from what can we *take* to what can we *give*. My parents reminded me that now that I was eighteen I was part of something bigger than myself, and that I could shape that something because I was no longer a child."

"Nobody makes a Will when they're eighteen!" Steve blurted.

"When I wrote my first Will, *at eighteen*, I left half my possessions to my only sibling, my brother, whom I believed could best use my money. I left the other half to a charity my grandparents had supported for as long as I could remember. Doing this had made me, my brother and my parents proud. Sibling rivalry was a foreign concept to us; still is, precisely because my family speaks openly and often about money. My parents always kept their conversations about wealth in perspective and nothing drives a healthy perspective more than the emphasis we all placed on our physical and emotional health – without that, monetary wealth doesn't matter.

"Everyone in my family has always shared the contents of our Wills with our beneficiaries. My first such discussion was a milestone, a rite of passage. When I shared the contents of my first Will with my brother, it was a moment that filled me with such pride and satisfaction. Our parents had taught us why and how to access the spirit of generosity deep inside ourselves. I can tell you, however, that at eighteen this generosity did not surface easily. At that age, most of us are focused on ourselves – it's all about us. *More* means more for us and we believe we're entitled to all we can conquer and acquire.

"So the generous spirit resided in me but only barely. It was only with my parents' wisdom that it was teased out and revealed through the exchange of ideas, not just once but every year when discussing my Will. It took me a full decade to truly understand that, like most people, my generosity had been stifled by a fear of death and that I was worried about running out of money and dying in poverty. And for someone in their twenties, it felt like that kind of death was a million years away and that only millions of dollars could fix it. It was only through conversation with my parents and grandparents about the possibility of dying with rich relationships that my fear of death retreated.

"Over time, that fear was replaced with hope and confidence that through hard work and good fortune, surplus wealth was the likely outcome of a life well lived. With fear cleared away through open discussion, I saw that the best lives are ones lived in collaboration with others. Family relationships and friends, not money, are the ultimate antidotes for the fear of dying. Family conversations – which don't cost a dime – are what put a great life and a great death within reach of everyone, regardless of how much or how little money they have.

"What struck me as odd the first time my father formally asked me a series of questions – seven in total – the first time he reviewed his Will after I turned eighteen, was why he had worked so hard despite his significant wealth, as revealed in his Will. But understanding this proved to be one of the most profound gifts my father ever gave me: learning that work can be loved, that it can and should be engaging and deeply satisfying.

"Most of the annual conversations with my parents taught me that the creation of wealth in the service of others, including family and the broader community, is more important than its consumption today. In a way, talking with my parents about the contents of their Wills every year was merely an introduction to a conversation about all matters relating to family and money, toggling backward and forward through time between my parents and everyone in the room, the past always informing the future, and vice versa.

"I saw every day the discipline my parents exercised by deferring consumption, denying themselves things they could easily afford. I came to understand that this delayed gratification was essential to compounding the growth of my family's fortune. This process evolved to become even more enjoyable than the consumption of wealth itself – that's a long journey from where I was when I was eighteen, when more consumption absolutely equaled more joy!"

"Oh, I dunno. Consumption's still pretty good," joked Steve, ostentatiously checking his Rolex.

William laughed. "Yeah, well now that I've turned 50, the concept of financial security and the *theoretical* purchasing power I enjoy is vastly more satisfying than the actual acquisition of more stuff that requires more care, more time, more maintenance and more energy. I'm not sure exactly when it happened, this progression to *less* representing *more*, but it's a milestone, a moment when wisdom reveals itself as a graceful, rich gift as we shift toward wanting to purchase more *time*, not more stuff. And I think some people only have this awakening before they die, when time is revealed as the great currency of life.

Steve was shaking his head. "Okay, this is all very nice for you, I'm sure, but how does this really work, in a practical way? A Will is an actual thing, you know, a legal document, not a state of mind."

"True enough. And in my family our actual Wills have kept pace with our state of mind. I updated my Will when I got married, updated it when each of my children was born, when I joined the family business and when the family business was sold. The family tradition of reviewing a Will on one's birthday makes sure they stay practical and legal and all that. But it's also a gift to myself to reflect on the great fortune and the challenges I've experienced over the previous year, and it's a reminder that one day others will take over my life's work. You see, it's not really just my Will, it's my family's and friends' and community's Will – it's more about them than it is about me.

"You'll like this bit, Steve – whenever I leave my lawyer's office, I feel a deep personal satisfaction that I've just taken **My Will is always done in collaboration with family** care of business, taken care of my family – just as my parents, grandparents and great-grandparents did with their Wills. My will to will is deeply satisfying because it is always done in collaboration with family."

Now Ashley spoke up. "Like I said, William – and Steve, I'm sure you can back me up on this – your family's approach to writing Wills is, I can only say, startling rare."

Steve agreed. "I've never seen it in my practice."

"But wouldn't it be great," Ashley said, "if this idea of transitioning from generation to generation and becoming self-sustaining could be reinforced not only in conversation but in practice by sons and daughters watching their parents embrace a healthy relationship with money? Parents who are neither in awe of wealth nor fearful of losing it give their children an extraordinary gift."

"And this idea of birthdays," Ashley continued, "it's fascinating. Are they not about measuring our progress through life? Don't we all approach birthdays with mixed emotions, especially as we get older? Don't we all have some apprehension, especially about those milestone birthdays, which can be a special reminder that we're nearing the finish line? It's the perfect day to think clearly about our Will, about who will inherit our things on the very day that people are giving gifts. I mean aren't they usually the same people – friends and family?"

"I don't know about you," offered Steve, "but I've never received a birthday present from a charity I've supported. Are you talking about a process designed to select beneficiaries that's lopsided in favor of family and friends over charities?"

"Absolutely not. When my parents go through the seven questions each year they use a slightly different version with the charities they've been supporting for years or new ones they're interested in. It's not a coincidence that both my parents began to receive some kind of birthday wish from a couple of those organizations after the process began. These weren't cynical gestures. The questions, and the dialog that ensues, really connect the donor and the beneficiary by establishing clarity around values about who my parents are and what they see their donation accomplishing. Charities that don't acknowledge a generous contribution while the donor is alive are unlikely to value that donor when they are dead.

"But it's more than donor recognition that I'm talking about. I'm talking about a charitable organization that, as part of its culture, understands that behind every single donated dollar is a story of struggle and risk. Organizations that make no effort to probe our personal narrative will never qualify for our family's financial support. If the cause is worthy, they may get our personal involvement so that we can work on changing the fundraising culture and value system from the inside out. But write a check to a listless, indifferent, uninterested, disengaged organization that approaches fundraising in a mechanical, impersonal way? Not in a million years.

"The questions," William continued, "seek to start an exchange of viewpoints between a donor and potential beneficiaries. But we know that every discussion takes two willing parties. Never confuse conversation with being lectured, hectored or controlled. These questions mark the beginning of our process of collaborative discovery.

"Now you would think that in my parents' case, when they sit down to discuss their Wills they would be the ones doing the talking, telling people how their money is to be used. Not so! My mother and father always told me, 'you have two ears and one mouth; use them in that proportion.' They heeded their own advice. They listen intently when asking the seven questions. Occasionally they might ask a qualifying question like, 'what do you mean by that?' or 'could you talk more about that?' These are always open-ended questions to tease more detail, more insight from family members, friends and charities they are contemplating leaving their wealth to.

"At the end of the questions, my parents would have a snapshot of who they were leaving their assets to. The smart charities have asked their own questions of my parents. The ones that didn't revealed volumes about themselves, about their administration, about their agenda. I think that generally, people are getting more sophisticated about their giving, wising up to the fact that just like people, there are organizations that do an exceptional job of meeting societal needs and others that... don't. Surely it behooves all of us to spend a little time to find the heroes among us – the family, the friends and the charities that will do something inspiring with our wealth, something more than just consume it. My family's questions have always helped us find the wisdom in ourselves and others."

"Never mind consuming it," said Ashley, "what about wealth left to people that ends up accelerating their demise by exacerbating their addictions, their laziness, their sense of entitlement? That gesture isn't a gift, it's a liability robbing the beneficiary of their integrity simply because the money came too fast and without context. And why? Precisely as you said, William. There's been no conversation, no connection established to the inheritance. It becomes silent money, awkward, guilty, toxic play money – call it what you want, it becomes a destructive force, not a creative one."

"Look you two," said Steve, "there's a simple reason why people aren't gathering around the proverbial campfire, holding hands and talking to beneficiaries about their Wills. Most people don't want to raise expectations with their family or whoever about what they'll receive when the person writing the Will isn't even sure whether their savings will last long enough to fund their own retirement. That's why they aren't talking about their Wills."

"That's an excellent point," remarked William. "If this is a fear then they also likely have fears about their care when their money runs out. But the sharing of ideas around a Will can be about giving *and* perhaps receiving – depending on when we die. Isn't it usually those we intend to give to who are most likely the ones giving their time to care for us, regardless of whether money runs short? If not, it ought to be something to consider."

"True enough," conceded Steve.

"Another part of your remark, Steve, is the presumption that we're all going to die old – that a Will is only for the division of old people's money and possessions," said William. "But I recall from my research for my first book that on average, in the US and Canada combined, more than 7,000 people die every day." He pulled his smartphone from his jacket and thumbed it quickly. "Here it is. Of those 7,000 or so, nineteen percent die in their nineties or older." He did a calculation. "That's about 1,330 people a day. Almost a third die in their eighties – that's another 2,240 a day – twenty-three percent die in their seventies and twelve percent die in their sixties. But get this: seven percent of people who die are only in their fifties and another seven percent are even younger than that – that's almost 1,000 people every day dying before we think they should.

"We all know the definition of old is a moving target," William concluded, "except that it's always at least ten years more than your current age! But look at how many people, on average, are dying before they're fifty, every day – an age we can all agree is not exactly ancient."

"A thousand people a day? I had no idea so many people died so young," said Ashley.

"Now we know that half of those 7,000 people will die *without* a Will. The half that *does* have a Will almost all arrived at their giving decisions without any conversation with family, friends or charitable organizations, in part because they figure death only happens when you're old. Their assets will likely transfer without guidance, purpose or in-

> As estates get settled, there is often more questions than answers

tent. As the estate gets settled and the checks get cut, there will be more questions than answers attached to that money and it may haunt beneficiaries for the rest of their lives. 'What did they want me to do with this money? Should I spend it? Save it? Is it really my money to consume? I know I didn't earn it.'"

"Ambivalence doesn't begin to describe the feelings many will have about that money," said Ashley. "I've spoken to friends who have inherited money and it's as if they keep a ledger in their head, splitting money and assets into two columns – one for assets earned through their own hard work and ingenuity, and the other for money that simply came to them as a gift – a gift tied to someone's death."

"That's interesting," said William. "I find myself doing the same thing. The more inherited money eclipses earned money, the more despondent and damaged the recipient's psyche can become, the more the inheritance can rob and undermine their true sense of self. In the absence of honest conversations before a gift is made, the gift is more likely to become the opposite of what most benefactors intend – it destroys potential as opposed to releasing it. Why? Because we give *in absentia*, we give when we are gone, we give secretly from the grave because of our own fear of death. We approach death with exclusivity and deny its implications for those around us. By doing so we can leave a legacy of confusion, guilt and depression, a method almost always repeated by the succeeding generation. The legacy of potential becomes one of despair.

"Ever wonder," William continued, "why some dynastic families seem to be able to make lots of money and keep passing it forward and growing their assets from one generation to the next? They seem to have a knack for growing their money faster than they add new family members. It's because they mastered *dying* long before they mastered investing. The planning for the transfer of assets begins as soon as the next generation is born. And by planning I don't mean tax planning – I mean a cultural education that slowly but methodically connects children to money, to philanthropy, to ideas and to a world bigger than themselves."

"But the über-wealthy," replied Steve, "have always benefited from their *consigliere* – their advisors and facilitators whose own financial success depends on the family's dynastic success."

"But why," insisted William, "can't a person with more modest wealth do precisely the same thing – prepare their beneficiaries to work for an idea bigger than themselves, their own family or community? This isn't a function of being rich or having expensive advisors, it's a function of people deciding to treat their Will as an opportunity to engage their intended beneficiaries and write the future together. The ultimate gift is a healthy discussion about the certainty of death and our preparation in every sense of the word for that day – whenever it arrives."

Ashley sat up, obviously putting the pieces together in her mind. "Oh my – it's never occurred to me before. I can't tell you the number of times a client in therapy has said 'what I'd *give* to have my mother, father, wife, husband, friend back for another chance to have a meaningful discussion.' Are they suffering in this way in part because of *how* their inheritance was left? The more I think about this, the more I think you're on to something, William. The real cost of unfinished conversations is unfathomable."

"Thanks for the encouragement, Ashley," responded William. "I'm really beginning to think a book is feasible."

"You better get writing," said Steve. "After all, you never know. Live every day as if it were your last, and all that."

"I think a better version might be, 'live every day as if the last has already passed,'" said William. "Seriously, imagine your last day has come and gone – what kind of relationships have you left behind? What are your regrets? Have you really summoned the courage to express your will, or have you left your family and friends with lots of unresolved questions? Have you left them fighting in court because you left your entire estate to just one person? Have you left all your money to charity because you made assumptions about the financial health of your children without really knowing? Have you left no money to charity even though you made public declarations that you would? Have you left all your money to your last caregiver because anything less seemed dangerous to your health? Was your last Will even your will, or did someone else hold the pen? The possibilities for dysfunctional, ill-conceived Wills are endless. Regret, anger and vitriol become the legacy of silence and the squandered possibility of building something more enduring than yourself."

"But I guess the feeling of half the population is, 'when I'm dead, I'm dead,'" said Steve.

"Precisely," replied William. "They miss the point that in fact nothing could be further from the truth. I'm not talking about religious beliefs here; I'll leave that to others to debate. I'm saying that whether you're Christian, Jewish, Muslim, Hindu, Sikh, Buddhist or an atheist, you will leave *something* behind for others to consider. Something *of us* lives on, something that was *in us* lives on in perpetuity and shapes our family, community, country and planet. What we leave behind, specifically our words and deeds, are magnified and examined for clues and hints to guide the lives of those we touched. But money is not on that list. Not even a dead billionaire's money will last as long as their words and deeds because the people influenced by that dead billionaire go on to live what they learned."

"Are you saying that the real issue is, what kind of clues about our real legacy do we leave? Are they cryptic clues and open to interpretation or are they crystal clear, documented, communicated and accessible?" asked Ashley.

William extracted the empty skewer from his cocktail glass and examined it. "When I read memoirs about the great figures who shaped our political, cultural and religious institutions, I want to know about their parents and the conditions that gave rise to the magnificent and audacious ideas that changed the course of history. I want to know about the confluence of events that gave rise to humanity's march forward. You mentioned Mother Teresa earlier. Well, I want to know about her parents and about Gandhi's parents, about Abraham

Lincoln's parents and John Lennon's parents, for surely their fingerprints are all over our history – a history that too often discounts the idea that greatness is born and nurtured, parented every day through words and deeds."

"We all leave something behind, even if it's indifference," Ashley observed.

William nodded. "When we invite our emissaries, be they family, friends or charities, into our conversations about the future, we take that exciting first step to see death as a huge opportunity to magnify our purpose right now – this is where our fear of death recedes, for it no longer feels like an end but the beginning of

> We all leave something behind ... even indifference

something bigger, more exciting and more enduring than a body that eats, sleeps and consumes. And if we don't do that, then yes, we leave behind indifference."

"When someone dies unexpectedly, say in a car accident at a young age, and we lament that they were robbed of their life, were they not also robbed of a good death?" asked Ashley.

"Absolutely," exclaimed William. "They were denied the time to talk and plan for the really big project, the really big thing that will change the world. Isn't this where the sadness sits? Isn't this where the *anger* sits when someone old dies without a Will, squandering their gift of *wisdom* and robbing the living of their purpose and themselves of a magnificent death?"

"It's a hell of theory, William," remarked Steve. "I suppose that when I consider some of the famous people who have died without a Will and, more shockingly, people like Leona Helmsley, who died with a Will leaving $12 million to her dog – named Trouble, no less – I can see your point. How pathetic that someone could believe that their dog could use their wealth to make the world better. What a mean-spirited statement to her grandchildren, to whom she left nothing. She thumbed her nose at humanity. She'll be remembered, all right

– not for her real estate savvy but for her vitriol, her disgust with humanity's potential. Not even dog lovers who take their pooches to Crufts every year would celebrate such a sad, distorted and angry gift. The interesting part of this case is that a judge later reduced the $12 million gift to $2 million. Her grandchildren, who were deliberately left out of the Will, were ultimately awarded $6 million from the angry Mrs. Helmsley's estate and $4 million was ordered to go to an animal welfare charity. Now you can be sure those grandchildren aren't going to go through life honoring the life and wisdom of their grandmother. What an impoverished family legacy."

"Yes, exactly," agreed William, excited that Steve was getting his drift. "Think of what $12 million could have accomplished for the hungry, the sick and the poor. Think of how Leona Helmsley could have lived on through the actions of others enabled by her money if only she had asked the right questions to help her begin a process of informing others of her interests. If those questions had revealed her abiding interest in animal welfare, imagine how much she could have accomplished if only she had started from a place of inquisitiveness, searching out solutions to the problems facing animals. That is a life worth living, not the mockery and disdain that made her the poster child for estate planning dysfunction. Like I said, whether we like it or not, we are all remembered for *something*."

Crunching on a piece of ice from her glass, Ashley turned to Steve. "Think about it for a minute. What kind of relationships will you leave behind?"

"Oh no, you're not going to put me on the couch, Doc!" laughed Steve.

Swiveling to face William, she pressed for an answer. "What about you? What are you going to leave behind? Are you going to leave more questions than answers for the ones you love? You and I know the people in our audiences are sophisticated – you better get your mind around this before you jump on planes and wing around the country helping people find their will to will, don't you think?"

"I know what he's going to leave," interrupted Steve. "He's leaving seven questions. What are they, damn it?"

"Fine," responded William, "but first, I need to visit the restroom. When I return I'll give you the seven questions. I'll caution you right now, though; if you think these questions are a panacea, you're wrong. They're just a starting place, a way to take a peek at our death and focus our energy on living today with the full knowledge that we came into the world with nothing and that we must leave with nothing. These questions use the inevitability of death to draw people together through conversation. It is only in the community of deep, trusting relationships that the real dividends of life are revealed. One dividend in particular stands out for me."

"Which is what?" pushed Steve, exasperated with William's deliberateness.

"We harvest what we sow." William smiled and shifted in his seat. "A great death comes at the end of a great life. The crop we harvest isn't adulation or fame, because we know those won't last and offer no respite from the fear of being forgotten. Rather, it's the acknowledgment that we will be remembered when our wisdom is woven through the lives of the people we touched. The giving and the taking, the good and the bad, the teaching and the learning reciprocate in perpetuity. When we receive care at the end of our life and die basking in the warm touch of our family and friends, we do so in the conscious belief that we will live on in their hearts and minds.

"Our perpetuity isn't secured by erecting memorials, because not even those will last forever. And even before that, the last person who met us and knew us will also die and our stuff – our businesses, our jewelry, our homes – will vanish. Our perpetuity goes beyond what we can imagine as those we shape with our words and wisdom today go on to shape others far in the future. My family's questions are centered on revealing our humanity – that's where great lives and deaths are conceived."

And with that William rocked back in his chair, using the momentum to spring forward and up out of his seat. "Hey, if you see the waiter I could use a black coffee."

"Yeah, yeah," said Steve. "Listen make it quick – at the pace you're going it'll take all night to get one question out of you, never mind seven."

4

Declaration of the Willing

Close your eyes and take a deep breath.
Now picture the birth of your child's child's child.

As he made his way to the restroom, William realized talking with Steve and Ashley had helped him think more clearly about the subject of dying and passing on wealth and wisdom. Conversations, he thought, are about ideas and about taking in someone's response to an idea. Conversations are about shifting, softening, hardening, giving and taking, usually leaving something bigger and more robust than what we started with. Conversations aren't about winning but about learning. They are reciprocal and, when carried out with intent, deliver exactly what had been received in that lounge with his colleagues – a reminder that we don't have all the answers, not even to the simplest questions. The wisest people, William reflected, seem to have the best questions, not the best answers – the hunt for wisdom is their defining quality. They are the ones who put the *why* before the *how*.

William understood the power of his family's seven questions to help shape dialog about two of the darkest and seemingly most dangerous subjects in people's lives – money and death. He knew from watching and listening to his parents and grandparents that confronting their fears wasn't a solo flight. Pushing through the hard stuff together created the conditions for opening up possibilities for a life well lived and for a death well conceived. By inviting others to fill in our blanks it was possible, he thought, for his family to relegate fear to where it belongs – shared with those who matter in our life.

As William returned to the table through the now bustling lounge, he could see Ashley had placed her notebook and pen on the table, ready to record his questions. He felt that same pang of responsibility he experienced when he approached the podium to speak. He was about to share wisdom born from his own family's personal and private exchanges.

The waiter took advantage of the break in their conversation to come and ask if they'd like refills. After he'd left, Steve leaned in, elbows on knees. Ashley smiled warmly, ready to receive what William had to say.

"All right you two," muttered William, "I don't want you to get your hopes up with these questions. Remember, the answers will change from year to year. The answers chart our evolution, our personal growth and the growth of our relationships with each other and with money and all that we have acquired.

"Consistency in holding your family meeting is crucial because people's wills change – by that I mean both their *Will* and their *will*. Remember I told my brother that he was the beneficiary in my first Will? Well, the week I was married I changed my Will and removed my brother. Not entirely – I did designate a number of items of sentimental value that I knew he would appreciate. But he wasn't surprised by this because when he and I had gone through the seven questions on my birthday six months earlier, he knew my life situation had changed because there in the room was my fiancée. Much had changed in ten years."

"Are you sure your brother wasn't miffed about being removed from your Will?" asked Steve.

"He truly wasn't," replied William. "I explained to him why I made the change and he understood completely – at the time he had been married for five years and understood my desire to take care of my wife should I predecease her. Two years later our first child was born and guess what, my brother is back in the Will as the guardian in the event that both my wife and I died. He was thrilled – okay, thrilled might be a strong word; he was honored. My wife and I knew he and his wife would make great decisions about our kids' well-being. I remember discussing that on my thirtieth birthday. Five years later, he took a job in Europe, so guess what, he was back out of the Will as guardian. You would not believe how quickly life changes and how quickly Wills become and remain outdated because people fail to meet, converse and update them every year."

"You're dead right – excuse the turn of phrase," Steve said. "I'd say this idea of updating regularly can't be stressed enough. It may seem like overkill but it isn't; a Will can become outdated so easily. I remember a law professor telling us that when Robert Kennedy was assassinated in 1968 his Will still named his brother John as executor, and we all know he had been assassinated five years earlier. And Robert Kennedy wasn't just any lawyer who ought to have known better, he was the damn Attorney General! We seem to be a culture that is *so* lazy or indifferent or cavalier, or something, that we simply don't keep our Wills current."

"Wow, that one takes the cake!" William exclaimed. "But this really does happen every day. Take, for example, a situation where the parents of two adult children told the kids that each would inherit fifty percent of the family farm. The children knew their parents' sizeable operation was worth about $8 million. Neither of the kids was interested in farming and went off to the city to pursue careers – one as a dentist and the other as an architect. Both were successful but not what you'd call independently wealthy. Both took on sizeable debts for their education and in raising their own families. They didn't save for retirement, believing their share of their parents' estate would coincide with their own retirement needs. Their parents even made them co-executors and gave them copies of their Wills. Time marched on. The parents ultimately died, of course, but it was revealed that they had changed their Wills. Voting control of the farm was given to a nephew who had taken over the operation of the farm as the parents declined, and *minority* shares in the business went to the two children.

"Turns out," William continued as the waiter arrived with their drinks, "that the Will had been changed *ten years* prior without a word to the now middle-aged children. The word eventually came down that the parents thought the kids simply didn't need their money because of their good careers. The parents felt that keeping the family farm in the family was the right thing to do. Here was a classic example of business owners dying and using their Wills to thrust children into business with each other and with extended family – the nephew. Now if you want to pull up a chair to a family reunion dinner, that would not be one of my first choices."

"Well, I can certainly understand why families don't talk about Wills," said Ashley, "especially if someone has declared a beneficiary and then removes or diminishes the amount they are to receive."

"These can be difficult conversations, no question," responded William, "but at some point the music stops and the Will is shared. If changes have been made in secret, expectations can come crumbling down and family functions become a contact sport – everybody lawyers up."

"Yes!" Steve said under his breath.

Ashley looked at him and raised her eyebrow.

"The genius of my family's questions," William continued, "is that these decisions evolve from the open sharing of ideas and never come as a *surprise* to anyone."

"Lesson of the day: Conversations ought to drive the changes to a person's Will, not assumptions," said Steve. "I get it!"

"Exactly," said William excitedly. "If you go on to use these questions with your clients, remember to encourage them to record their answers and to review them each year prior to asking the questions again. Remember, as advisors, you can only put the questions into the hands of your clients. You can't offer clues to the answers. The moment you do, you steal something from them and from the process. The value is in the struggle, the awkwardness, the tension and yes, maybe even in the silence, that the questions evoke."

"That… would take some getting used to," said Steve.

"I imagine it will," replied William, "but trust the process. These questions work. You must, however, remind your clients that when a question remains unanswered, that too is an honest answer. If someone finds one of the questions unanswerable, this is precisely where the fear and equivocation resides, and this is where trust needs to be built. The silence is where the real opportunity for conquering fear sits. This is especially true for someone who refuses to answer *any* of the questions – flat out refuses to sit down and talk about money and death. If we don't have an answer, we have an entire year to think, talk and search for wisdom to inform that answer in the future. Uttering the phrase 'I don't know' is one of the most powerful sentiments there is. The potential for personal growth and growth in our relationships lies in what we do *after* those words are spoken.

"Let's say, for example, Steve has a client –"

"It's not hypothetical, you know; I do have clients!"

"– a client who has no Will or has an outdated Will and Steve says something to the effect of 'I would recommend that you gather all your intended beneficiaries together and ask everyone these seven essential questions. They can be directed at family, friends or charitable organizations, and I think you ought to ask these questions before you write or update your Will.'"

"Okay," said Steve. "That's doable."

"Let's say the client, a parent, invites one of his or her children to answer the questions and they refuse or make excuses and find a thousand reasons not to talk – this informs the relationship. Encourage your client to keep extending the invitation to this person. They should never give up on family they believe can improve the world with the money and wisdom they intend to leave behind. Children especially will often refuse to speak with their parents about Wills, and this refusal is often misinterpreted. Some children are as gripped by the fear of their parents' death as they are by the fear of dying themselves."

Ashley added, "No question, especially when one parent has already died. The isolation and fear of further abandonment can numb an individual. It is remarkable that, even when there are great geographic distances separating parent and child, the very fact that parents are alive is like a warm bowl of soup to the soul. The idea of having to grow up because you are alone in the world, *parentless*, either becomes an opportunity to grow or it becomes an inflection point where adults wilt in the face of their new responsibilities. So I think what you're saying is that what we become in the face of our parents' death is shaped by our anticipation of this event. We move toward it through conversation, seeking wisdom from our parents who themselves endured the transition, or we turn away as if such transitions won't happen if we simply ignore them. It's a choice."

"The queen is dead; long live the king," offered Steve.

"Not exactly what I would tell a client," responded Ashley, "but yes, sadness and mourning over our loss of a parent can eventually be replaced by our hope for the future. The rhythm of family spans decades. It's easy to see why many don't notice the rhythm because of the long periods of silence between the painful thud of the drum with each family member's death."

"I suppose," offered William, "that the thought of being left alone in the world is excruciating. In some cultures, when parents raise the subject of their Will, children will shut down the conversation as a sign of respect, as a demonstration of their love of their parents and their indifference to the money and possessions that will be passed to them: 'If we don't discuss who gets what when you die,' they think, 'if we protest at the very idea of your death, you will see that we love you,' or so the logic goes."

Steve nodded. "I've seen that routine."

"I'm not surprised," replied William. "Of course, it's only after parents die and children receive their inheritance that regret at not having had the discussion and gleaning their parent's wisdom can consume them. It's hard to undo the past. There is an element of disingenuousness to this little routine that is usually revealed when parents who have died fail to meet the expectation of their children with respect to the division of their wealth and their possessions. The refrain 'how could they be so unfair, when I showed them how much I loved them by refusing to speak about dying, death and their Will.' It is the ultimate fuzzy logic.

"So I encourage both of you to guide your clients to persist with their invitations to family and friends to answer the questions if they run into this problem. There is one caveat: charities. Reluctance by any worthy cause to meet and discuss a potential gift, without any reference to the size of the gift, says volumes about the values that drive that organization. Unlike family and friends, who have a long and deep relationship with you, charities are in the business of soliciting funds with the view of accomplishing some benefit to the community. As we go through the questions, I'll talk about how my family uses a different version of the questions to determine which organizations to support while we are alive and as we prepare our Wills.

"There's something else you need to know about the questions. They are answered by everyone – by the person writing their Will and by intended beneficiaries. It is the sharing and comparing and contrasting of answers that leads to a conversation about inheritance and death. The questions can't be about someone exercising power and control by saying, 'I have these questions, now give me your answers. If you give me the right answers I'll give you my money.' That would be missing the point by miles. This is about working from or moving to a place of trust where we imagine relinquishing our possessions. To do that, we need to begin relinquishing our control today.

"Note that I said relinquish control, not abdicate control. I'm not talking about giving away money while you're alive, although some may decide to do precisely that after asking the questions and sharing thoughts. I'm talking about the *imagined* idea of having no money – having nothing at the moment of death.

"Steve, picture what that looks like – really looks like. Where are you? What are you feeling when you have nothing? Imagine relying on someone for care, totally dependent, in a place where money has no meaning. Now go a step further and imagine that the person providing this care is someone who is about to receive nothing, or something materially less than they expect? How do you feel? Do you care? Do you feel uneasy with the choices you've made? What does a loss of control feel like for you?"

Put on the spot, Steve shook his head and leaned back in his chair. "Yeah, I'm not digging that picture – we begin life wearing diapers and we end it wearing diapers," he replied grimly.

Ashley was sipping her club soda and just barely managed to avoid choking on it. "Where do you get this stuff?" she said as she dabbed her face with a napkin.

Bringing the conversation back on track, William implored, "Listen, the reality is that this is precisely what most people's death looks like. For those who can't summon their will to write their Will, or for those who have kept their Will secret, the moment when control transfers can be magnificent or tragic – it is a choice we make *today*. Just one more choice we exercise, or not."

"Something tells me you're going to tell me there's a catch," moaned Steve.

"You bet there is," replied William. "Death is an appointment, only we're never given the date or time. Like every appointment, whether it's going to the dentist, to work or meeting with a lawyer to write a Will, we are either early or late – there is no such thing as being exactly on time. You are on one side or the other of that precise second. Being on time is a myth."

> Being on time for death is a myth — you're either early or late

"So the idea of planning for your death, planning to be exactly on time for death, is an equal myth," said Ashley.

"Exactly," replied William. "You're either early or late. It's a choice we all make. And by *not* making a choice, we make a choice – to be late. 'They'll be late for their own funeral' is something we say to mock those who lose track of time. Those who die without a Will or a badly outdated one are late for their own death and mock their own life and legacy, because their time, they believe, is worth more than others'."

"No question," agreed Steve. "My experience has been that those who don't write a Will, or those who die with outdated Wills, will be remembered for how indifferent they were to other people." He paused to consider. "I'll speculate that my clients who refuse to use your family's seven questions to start a conversation with their beneficiaries will be the same ones who are late for appointments, not once, but habitually. I'll bet they're the clients gripped by a profound fear of dying, an appointment they want to skip altogether."

"And good luck to them with that," laughed Ashley.

"Another thing," said William, rather too loudly, as if he needed to really emphasize his next point. "Ever heard the expression 'controlled from the grave'? These are the folks who never let go of the idea of controlling people and money, even after they die. These are the folks who try to secure their immortality, not by inspiring the hearts of those they love, but by *controlling* them."

"How so?" asked Ashley.

Before William could answer, Steve interjected. "By using incentive trusts that effectively say, 'if you do X, I'll give you Y.'"

"I can guarantee," said William, "that the seven questions will be challenging for many of these people, as they are for all of us. This need for control comes from a place of fear and it seldom works. Folks who will from the grave will only be remembered for the fear that gripped them right to their death, and the fear they bequeath to the living as they try to hold onto them with their money. There's a theory that says children who grow up *fearing* money become adults *controlled* by money – a repetitive circle of fear that diminishes a person's spirit."

"I have to tell you," said Steve, "I see more people writing Wills and setting up trusts who say 'if you do this or that, I'll release some money.' You wouldn't believe the detail that people include in a Will in an effort to control family from the grave. I'm not talking about millionaires here, but everyday people who write Wills and include the strangest conditions, like, 'if you take your mother's garbage out every Wednesday morning before 9:00 AM the executor of my estate has been instructed to release $1,000 each year upon receiving evidence that said task has been completed.'"

"Wow," said Ashley, "talk about a lack of trust in *that* family. Have the kids been so irresponsible that they need a financial incentive to brush their teeth even though they're in their forties or fifties? Where do you draw the line in putting incentives in a Trust? Does stuff like that happen because the person dying really wants everyone to remember that they're still in control?"

"Oh they'll be remembered, all right," said Steve, "at precisely 9:00 AM every Wednesday, but not fondly."

"It strikes me," William said, "that incentives are created to encourage people or organizations to act in a certain way, without describing *how*. In the context of a Will, take a father who says, 'To my son I will release $100,000 a year for every year that he provides care to his mother.' Seems reasonable, but maybe not."

"How so?" asked Ashley.

"Well, let's say Junior follows his father's wishes and cares for his mother, to the point of keeping her alive on life support – against *her* stated wishes – because he feels he has a greater obligation to respect his father's wishes (and his money) than his mother's. Do you see how incentives can also be created *unintentionally* and can have unexpected and *negative* consequences, especially when there has been no dialog and when trust is in short supply? Unintended consequences happen every day when people try to exercise their will from the grave by doling out their wealth after they're gone."

Ashley nodded. "I guess people who can't relinquish their hold on their possessions before they die haven't built enough trust with their family to say, 'my work here is done, now go forward with my wisdom – and my resources.'"

"Nicely put," replied William. "Trust and respect with regard to providing care are inspired by ideas and ideals, not by the promise of money. The promise of money on its own without any context is simply a hedge by someone that *control* – the thing that works in life and in business – will work when dying. It simply can't, precisely because dying is the ultimate *loss* of control."

Ashley became excited as she put the pieces together. "So with your approach, people can get a taste of giving up control: ask the questions and try it on – what do you *hear* and *feel* when you imagine you have nothing but the trust of others?"

"Yes, precisely," replied William.

Steve said, "I don't mind saying how much anxiety about my own death I've been feeling during this conversation. But I can actually feel it dissipating a bit just talking about this now. I'm getting the importance of these questions. Have I mentioned that you haven't actually told us what they are?"

"Why yes, I think you have mentioned that," laughed William. "So let me tell you the first of my family's questions – right after I tell you about what my parents like to call their *Declaration of the Willing.*"

"That sounds a bit ominous," interjected Steve.

"Not at all. It's just an introduction reminding us why we're having our family meeting." Clearing his throat and sitting up on the edge of his chair as if to make a speech, William said, "this is essentially how we start the exchange of ideas about our Wills on our birthdays:

"Before we begin our conversation, I want to acknowledge that at some point in our lives we both receive wealth and give wealth. I use the word wealth in the broadest context to include money, possessions and wisdom.

The questions I am about to ask, and answer myself – as someone with assets and wisdom to share – I hope will be the same questions that one day help guide your own giving decisions.

The purpose of these questions is not to control who you are or what you become or even how you may one day use the wealth I leave you. Rather, I hope the questions and the discussions stretch our collective imagination about possibilities.

There is much I can learn from today's discussion. My hope is that the questions will help broaden and deepen our relationship, for I believe we can learn and grow until the moment we die.

There are no right or wrong answers to these questions, just an exchange of clarity and wisdom. These questions seek to begin a conversation about how best to use the financial resources and wisdom I have acquired to make a difference in the world. To do so, I will need your help, for one day I will die.

These questions aim to connect you to my money and possessions, not bind you to them. The questions will inform and remind you how my wealth was acquired and the responsibility that comes with inheriting wealth and ideally growing it for the benefit of others – for one day you too will die.

I need you to understand that you are my legacy, not my money and possessions. For my legacy to flourish, you must risk something, create something and contribute something unique and authentic to yourself.

This is all I ask. I hope these questions will spark thinking and sharing of thought in that direction.

While I'm alive, however, I would like our conversations to move us closer together. I believe that for this to happen, we should talk about what I will give you and how you believe you can receive it and use it when the time is right.

At some point in my life, I may require your assistance when I am no longer able to communicate. The conversation we are about to have will help us both prepare for that day so that we can all make informed decisions. I believe that the trust we build together talking about life and death is important.

The question remains: What will I give to you and what will I give to family members, friends and to charity? I believe it is only through conversation and transparency that we can arrive at the best decisions for all of us. My ultimate intention is to leave relationships that work well without me, and people who thrive in the company of each other because we have built our lives together with purposefulness.

It is in this spirit that I would like to begin our discussion. Before I proceed, do you have any questions?"

Shifting back in his chair, William ran his hands through his hair, locked his fingers behind his head, and sighed. "More or less, that's it – that's how our family meetings start. And notice that before asking the seven questions, we ask others whether they have any questions."

"And do they, usually?" asked Ashley.

"In the early days I sure did. Remember, I was eighteen when I started hearing this, so I'd protest and say things like, 'why do we need to have this stupid family meeting – you're not dying, are you?' I remember my mother answering that question casually without any hesitation: 'Why as a matter of fact I am dying, and so are you.' It wasn't a drama-filled statement, just utterly straightforward. I can still see her amazing calmness as she spoke. To this day it's oddly reassuring, a tonic that only a mother can offer, an idea that will be with me to the end – my end."

After taking a sip of his coffee, William continued. "After a couple of years I kind of knew the drill and we'd just dive into the questions. I do remember in my mid-thirties asking my mother whether she had ever shared the questions with a good friend of hers who had recently died. I kind of had a hunch that she had. I remember attending the funeral with my mother. Her friend had died unexpectedly, but I sensed from my mother's demeanor that day that the seven questions had made death accessible, for her sadness was softened with a kind of optimism and hope. She sure wasn't debilitated by grief, rather more informed by it."

"That's an interesting way of describing grief," said Ashley.

"In a peculiar way," continued William, "my mother had to be mindful of not looking too indifferent to her friend's death out of respect for others, whose inconsolable crying was, and usually is, measured proportionately as love. More tears equals more love. No tears or even worse, joy and celebration, equal no love, no compassion, no respect and certainly no grief."

"That's simply a cultural response," said Ashley.

"Agreed," said William. "We've all seen it. We're at a funeral and someone's public display of grief seems out of proportion to their relationship with the person who has died. My mother explained that sometimes people experiencing death confuse it with their own fear of dying. She reminded me that even that explanation was too simplistic. Those debilitated by grief, she said, are confronted with the brutal fact that the time for talking has come and gone. Questions that were once deemed off limits are suddenly crystal clear to the bereaved. But now the answers are irretrievable. Isn't that what's so terrifying and sad? And that's something to mourn, because our life is forever diminished by what could have been learned.

"We hear the phrase, 'we mourn the loss,' but my mother explained that though her friend was dead, she was not lost. My mother knew exactly where her friend was – she was in her heart and in her mind, precisely where both intended the other to be. Now that is a treasured gift, a more gentle grief to consume and learn from. Everything of importance that needed to be said had been said when exchanging the answers to the seven questions. My mother's grief could be described in a lot of ways but *regret* wasn't one of them."

"Wow, I get the feeling your family deals with death like an oil change – routinely, efficiently and without a lot of drama," said Steve. "You realize most of us aren't really like that?"

"I suppose when death is discussed and not avoided," replied William, "it does become kind of okay. We just acknowledge the *necessity* of death and it simply becomes a matter of fact – a fact of life.

"But here we go," said William, moving on. "So after that declaration, we dive into the questions. One year we spent three hours answering the questions and in other years, in fact most years, we fly through them – I think our speed record is thirty minutes. You'll see how that's possible when you see how straightforward these questions are. Especially question number one. Ladies and gentlemen, grab your pens."

"Someone call 911," begged Steve. "I think I'm going to have a heart attack. He's actually going to give us the first question!"

5

Tell Me a Story and
We'll Invent the Future Together

*Close your eyes and take a deep breath. Now imagine the death
of your child. Who's holding their hands?*

Preparing himself by draining his coffee cup, William announced,

Question #1: What word best describes our family?
Share a family story that helps explain the word you selected.

"That's it?" asked Steve.

"What were you expecting?" replied William.

"I don't know," answered Steve, "but I'm not sure how a question this basic is going to help someone write a Will. I mean, how can asking someone to pick a word help you decide who to leave your money and possessions to?"

"That was my reaction the first year I answered the question on my father's birthday and then six months later on my mother's birthday. A couple of months after that, on my nineteenth birthday, my parents gave me a present. It was a card with two words written on it – *love* and *trust*."

"That's a touching story, but…" Steve raised his shoulders, questioning.

"It's a touching story because *love* and *trust* were my first two answers," responded William. "Inside that card was a check. And on every birthday since then – thirty-one in total, ouch – I've received two gifts: one, a check and two, a birthday card always signed the same way, '*With love and trust, Mom and Dad.*' They truly heard my answers – their cards are proof. I can tell you that over the years, I've often used those same two words to answer that first question – that in itself is interesting," offered William. "But for me, more interesting are the words that only popped up once. Like *perseverance*, the word I selected the year my father and I worked incredibly hard to sell his business. Or *supportive*, the word I chose after completing my doctoral studies – something I simply couldn't have done without my parents' financial assistance."

"I can see what this question is accomplishing," said Ashley, nodding.

William continued, "It's important to remind clients who use these questions to write down their answers, to save and review them. The past can be a great teacher and predictor of the future.

"This question also asks for a short family story to highlight the word selected. And remember, the person who's asking the question, the person considering their Will – they answer the question and share a story as well. This exchange is fascinating. Of all the interesting narratives we can select, it's interesting to see which stories people choose, which ones we elect to pass on to our children. It's akin to the kind of storytelling that takes place at funerals, with the one obvious exception that we're all soaking up the best of family because we're still alive."

"Quick question," interjected Steve. "These questions – did your mother and father ask them one-on-one with each beneficiary, or was this like one big family meeting?"

"In our family, it's the more the merrier. This process is about unveiling secrets, not creating them. More people equals more sharing. We've also included spouses as soon as they entered the picture. Because the questions are asked on someone's birthday, we're all gathered for a dinner or celebration anyway, so what better way to focus on having fun than by reminding ourselves that one day it will end?"

"That just seems so counterintuitive," replied Steve. "Dying and death are depressing subjects."

"It is indeed counterintuitive, but the questions bring an urgency to the party, making the presents more genuine and the cake a little sweeter. Some years there are more people in attendance than others, but it's very much designed to drive openness, trust, creativity, awareness and purposefulness."

"This is going to be a real challenge for some people," Steve said, not letting William off the hook, "who think their birthday is all about having fun. They don't want to be reminded how old they are. Death's a huge downer."

"It is what we make it," replied William. "The way we approach birthdays is culturally informed. And right now the narrative holding sway is the one that says, 'have fun,' not 'have fun because one day you will die.'"

"I believe most people do think fleetingly about death on their birthday," Ashley said, building on William's thoughts, "but they don't formally acknowledge it. Birth and death are connected; our birthday is simply a reminder."

"Anyway," said William, "I can tell you, the routine of those meetings has made the idea of death itself so utterly routine – what a gift that has been. Contrast that with a family who doesn't have family meetings, doesn't share thoughts about death, doesn't have Wills and perpetually buries their heads in the sand."

"They would be the ones," Steve blurted out, "who say, 'talk about my Will on my birthday – are you nuts? Talk about dying and who gets what – what a downer!' But maybe a lot of parents would be relieved to find out just how much goodwill there is among family if someone could just take that leap of faith and begin the conversation."

"Those living in silence who can appear to be thoughtful and considerate can actually be creating the potential for family breakdown and breakup, like a free-for-all fifteen minutes after the funeral – or maybe even sooner, at the hospital, where someone lies in limbo as their family fights over whether to pull the plug or not."

"That's a good point," said Steve. "We haven't even talked about advanced healthcare directives, living wills – you know, communicating with family about how we want to die."

"There's no better time," William said, "to discuss resuscitation orders and the like than when family gathers to talk about a Will. In the absence of those conversations everyone will have a different take on what's right and what's best for you. Why not discuss end-of-life scenarios now, when everyone can hear *your* view, the view that actually matters, with everyone witnessing your plan? One-on-one chats with family might feel intimate, but there's nothing like having six different versions of the same conversation to cause confusion. A family meeting with everyone hearing and discussing your plan at the same time is clearly a gift you can give and enjoy."

"I absolutely agree," said Ashley, "because in the absence of deep and deliberate discussions about holdings and the end of life, the two will mix like oil and water at the most inopportune times. I once sat beside a doctor on a plane who, after I told him what I did, shared stories about families fighting in his hospital hallways, screaming and shouting, trading invectives and threats, mixing issues of money and care with no shame and no respect for their parent or even their own children, who watched and listened, possibly thinking, 'I guess this is what death brings.'"

William said, "It's a dismantling of the family simply because dying and death have never been discussed. Through their silence they leave a legacy for family and friends to gather and say, 'no Will, no Power of Attorney, no advanced directives – nothing! What the hell was he or she thinking? How could someone so smart be so irresponsible, so negligent and so naive?' Isn't this how so many of the living speak of the dead?"

"My experience," offered Steve, "is that those people heaping the scorn and criticism on the dead for their lack of planning have no Wills themselves, or have hugely outdated ones. They don't hurriedly get their affairs in order when this happens either. They don't run to their lawyer's office the day after the funeral and say, 'I've just had a loved one die without a Will; what a mess. I need one fast.' Nope, they dillydally and do what most families do – as you said, they repeat the past. Even people who do address the need for a Will don't call a family meeting to solicit ideas to avoid a repeat of the acrimony around a death. At least not in my experience."

Ashley remarked, "It's like there's a powerful force preventing us from *learning* from our own emotional experience such as when a loved one has failed to communicate their wishes. The thinking seems to be that if we leave death alone, it will leave us alone."

"Okay," said Steve, "I can see the benefit of this first question. It's a gentle question that gets the ball rolling and gets people thinking about the family and reflecting on the past."

"Absolutely," responded William. "The storytelling with everyone present is how family lore is created and perpetuated. People recall stories about vacations and important events and moments, times when the family came together and experienced something collectively. What better gift to give on your birthday?"

"Do these meetings really need to be on your birthday," asked Steve.

"Not at all. For us, birthdays work really well, but I have friends who hold family meetings on other significant days, like New Year's. That's another reflective holiday that measures our march through time. I have another friend whose entire family gathers a couple of days before Thanksgiving for their meeting. Now that family really puts the *giving* into Thanksgiving. Their meeting is long, detailed and capped with a celebration and a meal, savored by individuals sitting around the table knowing – not guessing – about the future. Their family plan has been built from the inside out and the outside in, from the top down and the bottom up, with equanimity, storytelling and sharing driving the entire event. These meetings include children as young as five sitting at the table, learning how to strip away the secrecy around money, understanding that money isn't mystical. It's something that's earned by risking something.

"Whatever day people choose for family meetings, it's important to develop a routine and a culture of consistency. For many, the predictability and repetitiveness of going over our Will is what calms the fear of death. So whether it's your birthday or the first Friday of May, make it non-negotiable, make it a meeting of such importance and stature that attendance is viewed as a matter of life and death – because it is."

Ashley asked, "And if someone refuses to show up?"

"In a way," William responded, "they *are* answering the questions. Their silence on the division of your estate should inform you about the health of that relationship. If someone can't show up because they have an emergency or can't afford to travel or has another legitimate reason, of course we make allowances. But a flippant 'I can't make it 'cause I'm going shopping with my friend' speaks volumes. Why would anyone leave money to someone who doesn't want to at least talk about what you're contemplating giving, about where it all came from and what it can be used for? So think about it. Will the quality of care you hope for later in life likely be provided by someone who can't be bothered to attend your family meeting for an hour once a year? The likelihood that that person will offer responsible oversight of your healthcare directives and charitable contributions is dubious at best. These are the relationships that require more work before naming that person as executor, beneficiary or guardian in your Will."

Pausing to clear his throat as if to make another important point, William leaned forward and said, "Okay, another little bit of housekeeping. Before we go much further I have to remind you to remind your clients that the order of the questions is important. This first question really sets the tone for the entire meeting."

"I'm glad you mentioned tone," remarked Steve. "So explain what happens if the person answering the questions doesn't have anything particularly nice to say. What if the one word that best describes the family is distrustful or angry, secretive, mean, cheap... I mean, it could be a long list, especially if this is the first family meeting and talking hasn't been a part of their culture."

"I suppose," sighed William, "the answer is what it is. If there is no meeting and there is no Will, the answer will still be the same. By understanding someone's ambivalence or hostility toward their family – getting it out in the open – the possibilities for addressing that concern and moving beyond it are vastly improved."

"Ahh, family relationships – exploring the really tough stuff! Now you're moving into my area of expertise," nodded Ashley.

"And that is precisely why I would encourage a family in that situation to look to you or some other advisor to attend that first meeting to get the family comfortable with the process," said William. "Over time the seven questions can be used to build trust and repair frayed relationships. Can you see how a process centered on a conversation about death and dividing assets can create the urgency to resolve relationship problems now? Death isn't a problem, it's an opportunity. The amount of money in someone's estate is seldom the real issue preventing this planning conversation from taking place. It's the health of the relationships. Procrastinate and the single greatest opportunity to deepen relationships by exchanging ideas and living a life with purpose in the service of others slips away."

Death is what we make it

"This is fascinating," said Ashley. "I would think that the conversations that unfold after someone shares a family story could lead to some interesting discussions, especially if the story addresses some negative family trait. But even tough conversations are better than a family remaining silent and simmering for years and then someone dies and the family heads to court."

"Now you're getting into *my* wheelhouse," replied Steve. "The number of families that battle in court, usually over money, and who air personal family secrets in public is alarming. Families in conflict have always made cheap reporting and entertaining reading. The curious sip their coffee and eat their toast intrigued by someone else's personal affairs splashed on the front page of their local newspaper – it's just human nature."

"Steve, I'm sure you'd agree that one of the biggest sources of conflict is when a parent writes their Will in secret and then appoints one family member, let's say the eldest child, to be the executor, gives that child a copy of the Will and that's the end of it, yes?" said William.

"Oh yes; I've seen that movie once or twice," winced Steve. "In many cases, the other children are told what's taken place, but aren't given copies of the Will and are left to make assumptions about who gets what, when and how. Many siblings assume that the executor is going to get more. The person doing the willing is blissfully ignorant of how they've driven a wedge between siblings; they just know that family dinners aren't the celebrations they used to be. Instead of creating a family that functions with trust, they've created one that turns on itself, through carelessness and indifference to people's feelings. This is a prelude to what's to come."

"I have to say, as an only child, I can only imagine these dynamics," confessed Ashley.

"Well, it's common," replied Steve. "The child who is appointed executor is often given instructions not to share the contents of the Will. In some cases, as bizarre as it may seem, some executors don't even have a copy of the Will naming them as executor. In many cases the person selected hasn't asked for the job and promptly proceeds to receive signals of mistrust and antipathy from other family members when their appointment is discovered."

"In our family," said William, "it is vital that people talk about the selection of their executor at their family meeting. Nothing can be gained by keeping this part of one's Will secret."

"But aren't we right back where we started?" asked Ashley. "Remember, this whole idea of a family meeting is foreign to most people."

"It is," agreed William, "and this is the culture we need to change. I'm not naive; I know the idea of sitting around talking about Wills is loathsome to most people or at best it's something they believe only rich people do to save tax. That completely misses the point I've been trying to make. No matter how much or little money we leave our children, or anybody, our ultimate gift is the conversations that come before."

"I'm not certain," said Ashley, "but maybe people don't call family meetings because they've never been to one and don't know how they work. I'll bet people have this idea that a family meeting takes place in an oak-paneled boardroom with a whole group of somber-looking advisors and everyone wearing their best suit."

"Some of the best family meetings," said William, "happen in kitchens, or on the back deck around the barbecue, with someone saying, 'I'm glad everyone could make it. I want to bring everyone up to speed on my plans. I've asked' – let's say John – 'to be my executor but it could just as easily be any one of you. It'll be a lot of work winding up my affairs and for this there is a small stipend reflecting the hours of work required to cancel all my utilities, file my last tax return, list and sell my house, deal with the lawyer, etc. But understand that you will all be treated fairly. I selected John because he lives the closest' – or he is a lawyer, or he is good at detail, or he's done it before; whatever. 'I did not select him because I love him more. In fact when my estate is all settled, he will probably be convinced that I loved him the least because being an executor is about as much fun as poking yourself in the eye with a knitting needle.'"

Ashley agreed, "I was the executor of my father's estate and that pretty much captures it."

"I think we can all agree," said Steve, "that the appointment of a family member, or multiple family members, as executor at the exclusion of others can cause great hurt and mistrust among siblings if not discussed openly."

"But I'll bet that *instinct*," said Ashley, "more than *fact* leads those not appointed to conclude that their siblings have out-maneuvered them, asked for the job, gained some kind of tactical advantage in getting a head-start in grabbing more stuff."

"My experience is that these folks don't know what the job of an executor is," said Steve. "If they did they would be thankful they didn't have to do it, especially if they don't have an aptitude for administrative detail. If people invited a trusted advisor to attend a family meeting to spend ten minutes describing the role and responsibilities of an executor, most siblings would be thankful that someone else stepped up to the plate to do a job that a lawyer will do but for a significantly higher cost to the estate. But the real point is that there should be nothing stopping a discussion about who is best suited for the job."

"So again, the lesson here," concluded William, "is that great family leaders take the time to educate their family. As a culture we are remarkably daft at schooling our children on how the whole dying thing works. It really just takes one generation to get the ball rolling. Once one generation sees how it's done, they can draw on their experience and really apply what it is to be a helpful matriarch or patriarch. As it stands now, we use those words to mean someone who

Great family leaders educate their family about money and death

is merely old, decrepit, cranky – and controlling with their money; someone who has more money than time. In the ancient tradition buried deep in our unconscious, before anyone had money and surplus wealth of any kind, we knew that matriarchs and patriarchs could teach us so much about living. As graduates of the school of hard knocks, they're the ones who have gained the perspective and have the clarity and credentials to share their wisdom."

"Getting back to business," Steve offered, "my advice is that those who are doing the willing better get this issue of naming the executor addressed. If they don't, then fifteen minutes after the funeral, all hell will break loose. I once heard about a funeral where only four people showed up: a brother and sister, each with their own lawyer. Now there's a picture for the family album. You just know that nothing we've been talking about, like the importance of family meetings and asking questions, ever took place in that family. Leaves you wondering what the guy in the casket could have done differently to leave a legacy other than two adult children ready to slug it out in court."

William nodded. "We're left wondering whether the two siblings had already learned that one was getting everything, or that they were getting equal shares of the estate even though one had spent the last ten years of her life providing twenty-four-hour care with nothing given prior to death to reflect that commitment of time and money. The scenarios that drive families apart after a death are endless, but the solution to such sad scenes is simple. It's not magic, just plain common sense that's within reach of every family prepared to sit down and talk."

It was Ashley's turn. "It occurs to me that several times this evening we have touched on this superstitious, almost mythical idea that people have about Wills and dying – I mean, you just used the word *magic*. A lot of research has been done about the origin of superstition. The theory goes like this: Babies, when they are needy – hungry, for example – cry. Magically, food appears. Babies come to believe they have the power to wish for something and it appears. Virtually every baby grows beyond this idea; as they develop into toddlers, people may ignore them when they cry or discourage the behavior, and the baby learns to abandon the idea that they possess magical powers. Abandon is a strong word, perhaps *shelves* the idea is more like it. Where they file the idea and how often they refer to it later in life reveals the extent to which *superstition* will dominate and inform their approach to life. People who gamble to excess often believe in their own powers, as do people who participate in extreme sports. And I propose that people who don't want to share thoughts with their family about their predictable death allow superstition to influence their idea of dying and dividing assets."

"Let me get this straight," said Steve. "You're saying our will to will is influenced by our earliest childhood experiences?"

"I'd go further and say that our death is influenced by our culture to the very moment we die," responded Ashley.

"And by culture you mean relationships?" asked William.

"Yes, relationships formed through talking," replied Ashley without hesitation. "From the moment we're born, our actions and words shape our attitudes toward death. The more we hear about death, the more comfortable we are with the idea. It's no different from anything else that causes discomfort – going to the dentist, giving blood, attending funerals. The more we talk about dying – and Wills – the more benign and uneventful it all seems."

"This reminds me of a story," said William. "I was at a funeral recently and the immediate family was cloistered at the front, separated from the other mourners. A moment before closing the casket, the funeral directors pulled a curtain closed so the mourners could grieve in private. Has this become our cultural response to grief – to hide it? Was the family self-conscious of their grief? Have we moved so far apart today in society that we cannot or are not allowed to share our deepest feelings through our presence and our conversations?"

"I suppose to really make this point, consider this," said Ashley. "The most excruciating deaths are the deaths of children. Difficult for parents because they never had a chance to fully teach and prepare their children for life or death. They feel their children are alone in death, inexperienced. This notion of preparing children for death is hardwired but we think the only teacher can be our own death, which the child will witness. When the natural order of our dying is disrupted, we grieve in such a profound way because it is the dying child who is teaching us about death.

"Paradoxically, many grieving parents go on to live the most inspiring lives because they have received a powerful gift of wisdom earned in the most incomprehensible way – they gain a rare perspective on living life with gratitude. It is not uncommon decades later, after wealth is accumulated, for parents to leave money to a charity in the memory of their dead child – in a way, acknowledging their child for the gift he or she gave them. It is amazing what our children teach us about ourselves – for example, when they show tolerance to others when impatience is our own defining quality, or generosity to someone in need when our own inclination is to hoard our surplus wealth."

Changing the subject as if the thought of losing a child was too much to bear, Ashley remarked, "Isn't one of the big lessons from your family meetings that every conversation between parent and child, between friends, is potentially so rich precisely because we don't know who will die first?"

"Exactly!" said William. "These meetings about Wills can be as much a gift to someone who may outlive someone younger in the room. We may think we know who's going to die first, but we don't. That's precisely why we ask our seven questions and seek and absorb wisdom in both directions, young to old and old to young. It's why in my Will, I leave specific possessions to my parents. They don't need my money, but a couple of items given with purposefulness will inform their grieving if I predecease them. A Will isn't just for the old, it's a document for the *living*, regardless of age.

"And remember that our family uses the questions to guide our exchange of ideas with all sorts of potential beneficiaries, including friends and charities. The *Declaration of the Willing* that we read before starting the questions is the same one read before speaking with extended family like nieces and nephews, friends and even charities."

Pausing to weigh whether he was dominating the conversation, William decided to share another story. "I remember a family meeting, I was maybe twenty-five, and my parents invited a local charity. A nice guy who ran our local community foundation attended the meeting. After some brief introductions my father explained that he had inherited a very deliberate and methodical approach to passing on wealth and wondered if the guy minded answering some questions on behalf of the charity; my father explained that he himself would be answering the same questions.

"The guy from the charity agreed and we got started. My father read the *Declaration of the Willing* and then asked him question #1, *What word best describes our family? Share a family story that helps explain the word you selected.*

"The guy sat in stunned silence and then admitted he didn't know anything about our family. My father said, 'no worries, you just met us, so let me tell you what one word best describes our family and then I'll tell you a brief story. The word I like the most,' he told the man, 'is *trust*,' and he told the guy a story about a scuba diving trip. My brother, father and I were eighty feet down and my brother ran out of air; we made it back to the top sharing our tanks. The man asked a bunch of questions and the connection began that moment, as he got a glimpse not only of who my father was but who we were as a family. Do you know that that man came back the next year and when asked that same question recalled that very same story and used the word *deliberate* to describe our family? Do you know how many other charities came back the next year and could recall the stories we shared? Not many, and that told us volumes."

Continuing the story, William said, "That man from our community foundation knows our family really well now. And we know just as much about the community foundation because of the twenty-five-year relationship we have forged in conversation with that organization. Now remember, when these questions are being asked, our entire family is in attendance; even my kids started sitting in on those meetings when they were five years old. They could write a book on what that organization has accomplished. When my father dies and money is left in his Will to that organization, it will be such a deliberate, thoughtful gesture, exactly the way he lived his life. Now that is a gift for us all."

"Well I can tell you, that is in stark contrast to most people I've written Wills for," said Steve. "I can't tell you how flippant most people are with those decisions. The gift is usually tax driven. And it's often given without a thoughtful connection to their family."

"So people will name a charity in their Will," Ashley asked, "and it will be a complete surprise to other family members when the contents of the Will are revealed?"

"Surprise is one word to describe it," answered Steve. "Nuclear bomb better captures the sentiment in some cases, especially when surviving family finds out that a charity is the sole or significant beneficiary. The mood can be incendiary, especially when children have provided some degree of care for their parents late in life. This doesn't serve the charity well either, especially when the Will is contested by the family, effectively pulling the charity into litigation. Families suing charities is one of the fastest-growing areas of estate litigation."

"It occurs to me," said William, "that I'm hearing a lot more people in my audiences say, 'I'm leaving the whole shebang to charity.' Whether they do or don't, this sentiment reveals the frustration and apprehension that people feel about leaving money to family, especially to children who, from the parent's perspective, will be 'ruined' when too much dough comes too fast. This sentiment is born from children whom parents see as lazy and entitled and whose consumption of an inheritance would be rapacious. It's become popular for people with lots of money, usually founders of successful businesses, to say, 'I'm leaving all my wealth to charity – my kids need to make it on their own, just like I did.'

"And I can see where they get this feeling," William continued. "Much ink has been spilled documenting the deleterious effects of a generation of weak, pampered, entitled children. Some would describe them as lazy spendthrifts who got too much, too soon, with too little effort and struggle. There is some consensus that the so-called entitled generation, slip-streaming behind the greatest wealth-creating generation ever, the Baby Boomers, is actually accelerating the decline in Western preeminence.

"No one can doubt the success of Western institutions – be they banks, universities, governments or media – at creating a culture focused on wealth and its accumulation. The rise of the entrepreneurial class, whose efforts have created financial success on a scale never before seen, has been pretty amazing. But the outcome of the 'more is more' culture is, in turn, also pretty obvious – bigger houses, more cars, more vacations, more of everything – except more time and more wisdom."

Ashley said, "I think those rants by the wealthy about their undeserving heirs are disingenuous and reveal nothing but short-sightedness. They just show how the great entrepreneurs make it all about themselves. Their egos leave no room for the luck and good fortune that was surely a part of their success. They also make no room for anyone, not even their family, to continue their work. In a way, their failure to plan for the transition of wealth could be as deliberate as their failure to plan for the transition of a business. If there is no plan, and the wealth is destroyed after the founder has died, then everyone will conclude how magnificent and talented the founder was. After all, he is dead and now so too is the dynasty and its wealth. Can there be any conclusion to draw other than that the success was all due to the founder's brilliance? It's as if they focus all their energy on earning and accumulating wealth, making no preparation for its transfer. There is no preparation of heirs. There is only one narrative: 'You want money? You better earn it, just like I did.' There is no vision for their money, just a singular narrative of the lone business warrior struggling to beat the odds. And so they leave it all to charity – their last lonely and angry act."

"I see this all the time," said Steve. "They can't see how thoughtless it is to raise children in the lap of luxury and privilege and then just turn off the tap when they're done using their kids as props in their own Normal Rockwell painting for customers and the folks at the country club. They don't gently break the news, but rather let their children hear from the lawyers that they'll get nothing. And as William said, that's the behavior the children will learn. All I can say to that person as they near old age is, 'I wonder who'll change your diapers, who'll really advocate on your behalf to ensure you medication is right, that the diagnosis is right and that the doctor's appointments are kept?' Do people really think some stranger will go the extra mile or will it be their family providing the care – the ones who were never good enough, tough enough or smart enough to 'make money they way I did.' Or is the whole declaration that all the money is going to charity a big sham designed to toughen up their kids, the ones who'll get a big surprise when they learn they've received a significant gift or maybe the entire estate?"

"What *is* that?" exclaimed Ashley. "I mean honestly; why the games when it comes to a Will and family and money? This nonsense of saying to beneficiaries 'you're in; wait, you're out; no, wait, you're in' grinds on relationships. The loss of the opportunity for a family to connect and accomplish something together is tragic."

"I'm sensing that we touched a nerve with this discussion," said William.

Ashley relaxed and sighed. "You did. My father, a successful industrialist, pulled the same stunt – told everyone, including me, that I was getting nothing in his Will. Then he died and left me everything. There are days when I want to bring him back from the dead and kill him myself. I have so many questions for him – do you have any idea how distanced I am from that money? The saddest part, I'm realizing tonight, is the lost opportunity for he and I to sit down and do what your family did, to think and plan and grow together, a father and daughter working on the greatest project of all, the deployment of his wealth. He was great at making money, but didn't have a clue what his money could accomplish beyond the obvious purchase of homes, cars and planes. He died with over fifty watches; I mean how many watches can one person wear? I can see now that he was absolutely stuck in his thinking and didn't know how to talk to me about his dilemma. He underestimated my capacity to live a purposeful life with the knowledge that one day his money would be mine."

"Not to diminish your story," Steve said, comforting Ashley, "but I see clients do this all the time – say one thing to their family and then do the opposite. I can see how your father's duplicity feels like a lost opportunity. It's as if people who do this want to keep their family on edge, keep them guessing."

"Or keep them controlled," said Ashley.

"Or is this an attempt to control death?" asked William. "Perhaps, as the end approaches, all the fear and thus confusion around death, relationships and money rears its ugly head. Without the benefit of time, energy and clear thinking, a last Will can make a mockery of last intentions."

"It's curious that you say that," interjected Steve, "because my observation is that Wills are frequently changed after a serious or prolonged illness. The longer someone convalesces the more prone they become to what I call 'inflationitis,' which can happen when someone who has had a long life, but whose last years have been solitary, has not been 'in the world.' They have their mental faculties but are not out and about in the world and lose touch with the cost of living. As they consider the division of their assets they look at their money using a very outdated value scale to guide their giving decisions. They may give $10,000 to a grandchild thinking this will pay for their entire college education, or give $250,000 to a local hospital thinking it will fully fund the building of a new wing. They leave their willing to the end and make it a solo affair. The results are usually disappointing for everyone, especially when an unspecified but significant balance is left to a single beneficiary, setting the wheels in motion for a contested Will."

"Also," said William, "without sitting down each year and writing their Will methodically and purposefully, people can allow their Will to swing wildly from one cause to the next. Impetuous willing as someone nears their end is common, especially where silence around money has defined the family's culture. For those who think money can buy a better end, it's not uncommon to see Wills changed frequently, particularly as one's health deteriorates. Virtually every lawyer I know has made trips to a hospital to do a bedside Will. How much fun are those?"

"They're brutal," replied Steve. "I'm liking the sunny scene you described earlier, on the deck around the barbecue. Every time I've had to go to a hospital to do a Will, it's the first clue that the guy lying in the bed has not brought up the subject of his finances with family. It's always a panic with relatives hanging out in the hallway, popping their heads in looking for clues about what they'll get. It's pathetic. I'm certain the last-minute drama doesn't add anything positive to the dying process."

"I have to believe," said William, "that the wild swings in sentiment of someone dying, from giving to family, to giving instead to friends, to instead giving it all to charity, serve no one well – especially the ultimate beneficiaries. When a family can build a *culture of willing* that is inclusive, informative, consistent and consensual, they offer themselves and their family a remarkable gift."

"Yeah – I'd call it the gift of no surprises," replied Steve. "This can be a gift more valuable than money itself. At least when there has been lots of discussion in the family about leaving the bulk of one's estate to charity, family won't have expectations that are dashed."

"It's for this good reason," said William, "that many financial advisors will caution children who say 'I don't need to save for my retirement because I know for a fact that I'm going to inherit enough money to take care of that part of my life.' Advisors see children removed from Wills all the time and financial plans come crashing down when there's no time left to save for their retirement. The more common scenario is when a parent dies and the value of the estate is vastly smaller than expected, ground down by healthcare and personal care costs racked up by living way longer than their advisors had forecast when they ran the numbers forty years ago. There was a time when people had a heart attack and actually died. Not like now, when they get a stent, run a marathon and live another thirty years. We are going to see people in their seventies taking care of their parents who are in their nineties – and older!"

"Correction, William," Ashley said. "We're going to see people in their fifties taking care of parents in their seventies and also taking care of grandparents in their nineties. Come to think of it, it's even tougher than that. With people having children later in life, people in their fifties are still taking care of their own children. They're going to be the luncheon meat in the caring sandwich, a triple-decker sandwich that's tough to swallow and digest unless the family can begin talking about their Wills, powers of attorney and advanced healthcare directives now – and as you've convinced me, every year."

Reflecting further on what William had said, Ashley added, "People change their Wills all the time, and depending on where you're sitting, it's a good thing or a total calamity. I guess we're saying, for goodness sake don't spend thirty years telling someone they're going to inherit everything, and then in the last month of your life change your mind."

"Hang on a second," interjected Steve. "What if the kids who are expecting everything are indifferent to their parents' well-being, showing all the signs of entitlement – you know, just rubbing their hands together waiting for the windfall. The parents have played their hand, revealed their plans. Maybe changing the Will in the last years of life will serve the kids right? Isn't this precisely why parents keep the contents of their Will secret?"

"In my experience," replied William, "this attitude just doesn't show up in children. If someone was really exploring their Will consistently every year, they would have unearthed this attitude along the journey of life. More importantly, maybe, just maybe, those annual conversations would have framed a different set of values and led to a different kind of relationship between parent and child and a different com-mitment to providing care."

"There's so much work to do when someone dies," Ashley pointed out, "that the last thing family and friends need is surprises. Not even good surprises like I had are truly gifts. Leaving a sum of money that is way beyond what was ex-pected can cause hardship of a different kind. I'm not sure if people understand how tricky it is to give money away, even to charities."

"It *is* tricky, which is why my father uses question #1 to show us how we could make charitable gifts as a family. We only give to organizations that truly understand who we are, where we came from, what we believe and where we want to go as a family. You'll see from some of the other questions what I mean.

"The first question is the first clue for a charity that when my father is dead, his family will be there to steward his gift, to oversee the work his hard-earned money is fund-ing. In our family, oversight of our charitable contributions is both a responsibility and a gift that connects us to him and him to us – the past intersecting with the future. We view our charitable donations as expenditures and with every expenditure we look for value. Our value of hard work carries through to our charitable giving, and our charitable giving drives our commitment to hard work. It's a reciprocal gift, just like the conversations leading up to our selection of a cause to support."

Ashley said, "I can tell you from my psychotherapy work that there can be such heartbreak and confusion when children are raised to be careful with money, parsimonious even, only to find out when their parents die that a charity that has never been spoken of receives a large portion of the estate. It makes a kind of lie out of the family dogma that money is earned, not given. Ask the administrator of any charity if they have ever received a large unsolicited bequest right out of left field. Most have, and most know that almost certainly behind every one of those gifts is a family scratching their heads, wondering equally what drove that decision. The sadness and anger lie in the fact that the gift could have included a rationale for why *that* charity, why *that* amount. But to die with such indifference to family by hoarding the wisdom behind the gift seems strangely sad."

"Correct me if I'm wrong," offered Steve, "but what you're saying is that when parents involve their children in discussions about their Will and the kids understand the logic of why a parent wants to leave something to a particular charity, the gift is *to and from* everyone in the family."

"You're starting to scare me," said William. "Yes, that's exactly what I mean."

"I can certainly now see how your family's first question can get people comfortable and at least starting to talk about death and dying," said Ashley.

Obviously wanting more and wanting it faster, Steve asked William, "Any chance you're prepared to share the second question?"

"Absolutely," responded William. "This question may surprise you. Remember, everyone in the room, including the person considering their Will and asking the question, answers the question. So,

Question #2: Describe how your parents acquired their wealth. Share a memory about something your parents did to provide for you that left a lasting impression.

"Note that this question asks how they remember their *parents* acquiring their assets," said William, "not how they themselves acquired their wealth. My father describes how his father and mother acquired wealth and I describe how my mother and father acquired their wealth. The storytelling again affirms and confirms something about our individual and collective memory of family and can be added to by everyone in the room. This repetitive storytelling is how we invent and imbed our family narrative and make it lore."

"Interesting," said Ashley. "Right out of the gate the first two questions involve storytelling, looking backward before you begin to cast your eyes to the future."

"Indeed," replied William. "Right up front in the process of considering your Will, ask family, friends and charities to reach back in time to recall and honor how someone acquired more money than they consumed over the course of a lifetime. This question, more than any other, uses the past to inform the future. It's a teaching question, in which respect for inherited money is earned and learned – more wisdom."

"Very cool," muttered Steve.

"More importantly," said William, "it shows how the concept of *wealth generation* varies from one generation to the next. The person writing their Will will see how different their life experience has been from their parents'. It plants the seed that their own children will also likely pursue their own authentic path."

"I love these questions," enthused Ashley. "I wish my mother and father had asked and answered this question because I have always wondered how my grandparents acquired their money. I have no idea whether they inherited it, earned it or won it at a casino. Consequently, I have no idea how much my parents' success was attributable to my grandparents and how much my grandparents' success was a result of their parents' help. We've not shared that piece of our family history and everyone, I think, is left with the impression that whatever success my father enjoyed in business, he did it all on his own. I can tell you he never went out of his way to dispel that notion. But that piece of the family narrative is now gone. With my parents dead, I can never know how much of his success and my success is really the success of our collective family history. I'm left wondering whether I'm part of an old successful family or whether I'm a successful individual. And for me, not knowing feels like something valuable has been withheld from me."

"In our family," replied William, "this question dispenses with the heroism and ego right up front and acknowledges the gratitude we ought to have toward our parents, even if what they gave us in terms of money was modest. We all came from somewhere. This gratitude informs our own giving. More importantly, it reminds us that not all gifts from our parents involve money. Arguably the more valuable gifts are intangible. Patriarchs and matriarchs are the keepers of family stories – it is their special responsibility to not just repeat the stories they have inherited from their parents and grandparents but to build on those stories and insert their chapter in the book of family wisdom. How else can we learn? Or do we not care if our progeny keep making the same mistakes over and over, the same ones our forebears made?"

"Not to put a downer on this whole process," Steve interrupted, "but what if, when recalling these family stories, the memories that come flooding back aren't great ones? What if, when you ask someone to recall how their parents acquired their wealth, they answer, 'they robbed banks.' How can this shape a Will in a positive way?"

"Because," said William, "we no more define ourselves by the bad than we can define ourselves by the good. The notion of entitlement cuts both ways. We are no more bank robbers or rum runners ourselves than we are successful entrepreneurs just because our parents were one or the other. Telling stories about how our parents acquired their money merely reminds us where we came from and gives us a chance to see the good and bad for what it is. It gives *them* a chance to share what worked and what didn't.

"When parents free their children to pursue their own path, it is a remarkable gift. We are emancipated, free to become who we are meant to be. The gift that parents leave through these stories is not 'how to become a plumber or a lawyer,' it's simply the respect they have for their children to pursue their own authentic passion. Henry Ford, Mary Kay, Ron Hewlett, Bill Packard and Steve Jobs all did work profoundly different from what their parents had done. The results speak of their families' efforts to raise inquisitive, driven and purposeful children as much as they speak of their individual efforts.

"I can tell you," William continued, "that the magnetic pull some children feel to do exactly what their parents did is profound – farming, retailing, landscaping, trucking, accounting, whatever. It's not a bad or wrong thing, but rather evidence of the highest degree that parents wield a profound influence on the choices children make. Whether we want to acknowledge it or not, children live what they learn and, as parents, we need to be mindful of this."

"Now that's about the fifth time you've used that expression – 'children live what they learn' – what's the deal with that?" asked Ashley.

"It's my all-time favorite poem. It's by Dorothy Nolte and it's called, *Children Live What They Learn*. Surprise, surprise. It hung on the wall of my grandparents' cottage."

"I'm, not familiar with it," said Steve.

"Look it up, man; I'll wait."

Steve sheepishly thumbed his smartphone, read, then handed his search results to Ashley.

"That's beautiful," she remarked. "I'd say the qualities mentioned in that poem – the good juxtaposed to the bad – are learned. Everyone starts with something. We are all products of our environment, good and bad."

"No question," replied William. "Some of the most successful entrepreneurs have come from the most difficult family situations. They see adversity in their work and it feels familiar; problem-solving is all they know. Equally, some of the most enduring families of fortune have mastered the process of raising intelligent, hard-working, creative risk-takers who understand that their responsibility is to take inherited wealth and grow it for the benefit of their own children and their community. They teach their children to find their own voice, find their own path and to do whatever they do with conviction. The idea of our children becoming replicas of us is dangerous in a world where change is constant. Why wouldn't we want our children to be so much more than ourselves?"

Steve said, "So while the past can inform the future, it's really more of a reminder about how we all need to adjust to change."

"Yes," said William. "However, I'm guessing we've all met people who have acquired significantly more wealth than their parents had. Some call them the *new money*. The problem often is that they have no historical reference for how wealth can and should be transitioned. They're looking for the perfect solution all on their own, and so they often end up dying without Wills. People referred to as having *old money* know that many of them have had the benefit of generations of conversations and a wisdom earned through a responsible engagement with money. There is a teaching and learning about risk and creativity. This is how new money becomes old."

"So this second question is going to get everyone in the room recalling how money was acquired," said Ashley, "and by recalling how it was acquired and how it was used to provide something for someone else, people can focus on what their forebears sacrificed to provide opportunity for others."

William nodded. "It's a great reminder for successful people that someone had a hand in their success. It's a question designed to extract gratitude from people prone to believing they did it all on their own. Gratitude needs to be taught and that is the purpose of my family's second question."

"And," exclaimed Steve, showing more signs of getting on board with the process, "the next generation may not possess the skill or luck to create the same wealth for their family."

"The truth is, some don't," replied William. "If all we pass on to our children is the idea that a successful life is measured exclusively in dollars, you can see why there is such incredible sadness, insecurity and regret among inheritors. Families who can answer this question honestly and openly learn volumes about how wealth and wisdom can be accumulated and about the role that luck, hard work and risk-taking play in creating wealth. Will the children of Bill and Melinda Gates go on to found a business and grow it to become larger than Microsoft? Not likely. Does this make these children failures? Of course not. Hopefully this family has passed something far more valuable than money to their children: the wisdom to be truthful, generous and authentic people."

"This resonates with me," said Ashley. "Psychotherapy couldn't be any more different from manufacturing. I always thought my father viewed my choices with some measure of disdain and regret. He made it clear that there was only one credible and honorable path – the path of the great industrialist."

"The one he took," said Steve.

"Indeed."

"When my father answered this question," added William, "he shared stories of his father's awful summer jobs, the risks, rewards, triumphs and failures, right up to the time he sold the business he built from nothing. He loved telling those stories and I loved hearing them because they reminded me that his father was a forty-year overnight success. Those annual family meetings gave me the encouragement to play the long game, to keep grinding through adversity to reach my own goals. When I answer this question, I have the opportunity to recall how my mother and father worked so hard to build and invest in a business they believed in. I can remind them of things they forgot. At the end of this question I always take away one fundamental teaching: there are no shortcuts to acquiring authentic wealth, be it money or wisdom. Those who take shortcuts – lottery winners, or those who inherit vast sums of money without any preparation or clue that it was coming – live tough, often dysfunctional lives, with their windfall stealing from their authenticity."

Unearned and unlearned wealth does strange but predictable things...

"Have you ever seen one of those documentaries that trace the life of lottery winners?" asked Ashley. "Unearned and unlearned wealth does strange but predictable things to people and their family – sobering stuff. I can tell you that despite my own privileged upbringing, I was totally unprepared to receive the kind of wealth I inherited from my father."

"So why do you work?" asked William. "Why do you negotiate the high speaking fees you do? And what about those rumors that you demand a fruit basket every morning when you're on a speaking tour?" he added with a wink. "What's up with that?"

"My lawyer has instructed me not to discuss the details of my contract rider, if you don't mind," she laughed before turning serious. "Do you know that were it not for my own therapist and years of hard introspective searching, I probably would have stopped practicing psychotherapy the day the lawyer called with the news of my inheritance. I mean, from that day on, I sure didn't need to work. Thankfully, I was reminded why I entered the profession in the first place. This is what drives me forward now. The speaking fee I earned today, like all the rest, will be donated to charity because now the game is this: How do I use the opportunity gifted by my father – financial independence – and my skills to move money from the companies that hire me to speak to my favorite charities?

"Money is still one of my focuses, but I can see the shift in its purpose. My father's money didn't make me lazy, it made me more productive. I think of my father every time I speak and so do the charities I support, for without his gift, my gift would never have been rediscovered – repurposed, if you will. I stumbled into this wisdom through therapy; it sure wasn't his or my plan. I know others aren't so fortunate."

"I think you're right," said Steve. "I can tell you that most of my clients struggle to talk about money. They just don't have the conversations. Money transfers like a smoking gun to children who will destroy themselves and their own families because silence is all they know. This idea that money can purchase slothfulness is a fantasy – one that lasts about two weeks, the precise amount of time it takes for the aimlessness to drive someone to distraction. I think we're all built to create something – be it a business, a social cause, relationships – something. Ask yourself this: Do billionaires *work* or do they *create*? If money was merely about consumption, billionaires would be the epitome of idleness and slothfulness and yet I haven't met one who isn't absolutely driven to keep inventing the future."

"The bottom line," concluded William, "is that everyone is rich when money, regardless of the amount, is earned in the service of others, ultimately for family, friends and humanity. Working exclusively for the idea that the money we earn will simply buy more stuff, and that more stuff is *more*, will destroy anyone slowly but surely from the inside out. Some learn this from their parents at an early age, others as their last breath nears."

With that the waiter arrived at the table and asked if they would like to see the menu.

Steve was the first to comment. "Well, it's 8:30 and we've only got through two of William's seven questions. I think we'd better order. I'm not letting him outta here until I've got 'em all."

Reaching for one of the menus the waiter had placed on the table, Ashley simply said, "Let's eat."

William was already scanning the menu.

Without looking up, Ashley said, "Go ahead if you're ready, William."

"Alright, I'll have the Caesar salad and the linguine."

Ashley didn't raise her head, so the waiter turned to Steve. "And for you, sir?"

"I'll have the soup of the day and the eight-ounce Porterhouse, medium rare, please."

"Very well," said the waiter, turning to Ashley.

"I'm going to have two starters, please – the house salad, blue cheese dressing, and the grilled calamari."

"And how about some wine?"

"Yes, that would be great," said William. "What do you guys think? A bottle of the house red? It's a Pinot Noir."

Ashley and Steve agreed.

"Okay," said the waiter. "I'll be back with some bread shortly."

"That has got to be the fastest anyone has ever ordered," observed William.

"Alright, are you guys ready for the third question? I'll forewarn you, it's a beauty. It cuts right to the core issue of how much money to leave, to whom, and when. Of all our family questions, this one is the hardest because, unlike the first two, it looks forward – it requires imagination, maturity and courage. Of all the questions, my answer to this one has changed the most over the years."

After pausing to allow some drama to build, William said, "Okay, here it is."

Just then Ashley spotted the ever-efficient waiter heading to the table with their cutlery and whispered, "William, give it a second, would you."

Looking up, Steve sighed, grinned and said, "Of course he's coming now."

6

Dead but Definitely Not Gone

Close your eyes and take a deep breath.
Now imagine… When the last person who ever
knew you has died, how will you be remembered?

When the waiter had gone, William said, "Alright you two, grab your pens.

Question #3: How would an inheritance advance your dreams for yourself, your family and your community?

"Okay," responded Steve, "now we're cutting to the chase. Although I have to say this question feels like it could turn into a bit of a competition, right? I mean, I'm trying to picture a family meeting with a bunch of siblings in the room along with mom and dad and mom is saying, 'Okay, tell me what you'd do with the money.'"

"A parent can turn this into a competition or they can set the tone and use the question to start an informed discussion about *needs* and *wants*. There are no right or wrong answers, just an opportunity to benchmark where a family member is in their evolution and maturity with respect to their relationship with money."

"Well, you know and I know," interjected Ashley, "that there is a huge difference between what we want and what we need. Is this question designed to expose the difference and maybe teach the family about money?"

"Absolutely. This question, more than any other, will reveal our relationship with money. The same applies to charities. Imagine inviting a charity to the family meeting and asking this question. Imagine how they would respond when asked how a gift of money or property would advance their dreams for themselves, their family and the community."

"I can only imagine," replied Ashley. "Remember, we never had family meetings." She smiled.

"Right. Well the first time we asked this question of a charity we could see how confused and uncomfortable the representative became. It's obvious they were uncomfortable answering the first two parts of the question dealing with their *personal* dreams and those of *their* family."

"It is a rather unusual question for a charity to answer," offered Steve.

"Oh I agree, but here's what we've learned," said William. "A charity, like any organization, is made up of individuals. These individuals are hired and trained to raise money or do other work for a cause. The ability of that organization's leadership to attract and retain exceptional people who are driven by a set of values will show up in how they answer this question. It reveals who we have sitting in front of us. Do we have a professional fundraiser trying to hit his or her number? Or do we have someone working for that specific cause because something stirs inside him or her to make something better, to make something right, be it a cure for a disease, relief of poverty – whatever. Who they are reflects who the organization is and vice versa."

Leaning forward and taking a sip of his coffee, William continued. "Remember the guy I told you about from the community foundation who attended our family meetings all those years? His response to this question the first year is one of the main reasons we invited him back year after year. When we asked how a gift would advance his own and his family's dreams and benefit the community, instead of skipping to the end and explaining the mission, vision and values of his organization (what we call the script – every charity has one), he dug into the first two parts of the question. He talked about how personally satisfying it would be to connect our family to his family. He explained that his family lived in our community and described how our money could lift them up, lift up the community that we were *all* part of. He talked in general about what community means and how we are all connected and then specifically about how our gift could directly improve his own children's lives.

"Now did this guy have our attention? You bet he did. He talked about how our money could be used to create green spaces for kids to play – his kids – and when he talked about funding breakfast programs at one of the local schools, he connected it back to his kids, who played with some of the kids who would use that program. We knew we had a winner. We knew we had a guy who would take our hard-earned money and treat it with the respect that gifted money deserves. Why? Because he was driven and shaped by his own narrative to improve something that he was deeply connected to – his own family."

"How did some of the other organizations invited to your family meetings answer this question?" asked Ashley.

"You wouldn't believe some of the appalling answers we've heard from charities over the years. One person was flat-out stumped by the question. When we contextualized it a bit, he actually said he would benefit personally because he'd earn a bonus by exceeding his fundraising goal. It was an honest answer to be sure, but clearly not the one we were hoping for."

"I love it," laughed Ashley. More seriously, she said, "I can see how a family that's meeting with a charity and hearing their response can pull everyone into the gifting process."

"Exactly. Even though it was my father or mother asking the question with a view to updating their Will, all of us in the room became engaged in the process. After the representative from the charity left, we'd talk as a family. My parents would ask us what we thought. We came together around the disposition of their wealth precisely because we were part of the process. Each one of us saw or heard something unique in the conversation with the charity that we highlighted and shared with the others. Consequently, we made better, more informed decisions through our collective wisdom.

"And this dilemma of selecting worthy causes," William added, "isn't just a process for the rich but for everyday working people who have a modest amount of wealth to pass on. These folks underestimate how even a small gift to charity can leave a big impression on children when they are included in that decision. Every family, regardless of their wealth, needs to have family meetings."

"It's so logical – such common sense," added Steve.

"It really is," confirmed William. "Each year my parents would ask us how comfortable we were in overseeing the gifts they intended to leave for various charitable causes. After witnessing the good, the bad and the ugly, we knew that oversight was essential if our family legacy was to be preserved. This responsibility has come to include sitting on boards and various committees while my parents are alive so that we truly connect with and understand what we're trying to accomplish with our gifts. When my parents die there will be no surprises about what causes captured their imagination or about what our role will be in honoring and supervising their gifts.

"This involvement in charitable causes sends a strong message to our own kids, who listen and watch how we discern a worthy cause from one that is not only bloated with administration but more concerning, one that is ineffective in meeting their stated objectives. Our children learn that a charity with eight percent administration costs isn't necessarily more worthy than one with fourteen percent. It isn't a race to the bottom in admin costs. We're looking for impact, results, outcomes – *effectiveness* is the word I'm looking for."

"Your family is definitely unorthodox," replied Steve. "Most people evaluating a charity look exclusively at administration costs. However, I see what you're saying. Without doing your due diligence you could be supporting a charity with a three percent administration cost that is doing little of substance with the other ninety-seven percent."

William nodded vigorously. "Question #3 takes the randomness out of our family's charitable giving and reframes it as a family project deserving of time and attention commensurate with the effort that went into making that money in the first place. Not to sound pious but our charitable giving is not tax driven, it's values driven, with an emphasis on need and effectiveness. Anything less mocks

Charitable giving ought to be *values* driven

those in our family who came before us, whose sacrifice, hard work and deferred consumption led to the donation. How we give informs how we earn and how we earn informs how we give. The charities that came to know our family came to know this about us."

"This is really interesting," said Ashley. "Shortly after my father died I was approached by four charities, all claiming to be my father's absolute favorite cause. Because I wasn't involved in his giving decisions, I had no clue what he had done or what he thought about these organizations. It was rather embarrassing to be put in the position, as sole beneficiary, of not knowing what commitments he had made. I totally fumbled through the process. I can see that my father missed an opportunity to use his money for us to grow together by working collaboratively on his philanthropy. The sad part is that I know how hard he struggled to make his money. That he just gave it away for tax reasons when he was alive without any discussions with me about what causes touched his heart is terribly sad – a huge opportunity lost."

It was Steve's turn to weigh in. "Ashley, imagine if your father's Will had gone the other way and he had left all his money to charity instead of to you."

"Well, I'd probably be giving you a call and asking how I could contest the Will," she responded. "My father was a difficult man – that I ended up as a psychotherapist should be the first clue that things weren't always easy between us. I loved him and provided care for him when he needed it, but none of it was ever easy. That he made me sole beneficiary certainly acknowledged what he felt for me – I think. Unfortunately it was the silence between us when he was alive that remains between us now that he's dead. William, I wish I'd met you sooner! I wish I had known about your seven questions and bridged that gap. I have such regret and it's such an unproductive and negative emotion."

Wanting to acknowledge the courage of her confession, William looked at Ashley and smiled, "You have an amazing opportunity in front of you. You can either repeat your experience when you update your own Will, or you can engage the important people in your life and invite them to your death *now*. Obviously we all hope that day will be decades away, but you can start this dialog today, using these questions. I know you don't have children or siblings, so who would you invite to your family meeting?"

Answering his own question to avoid putting Ashley on the spot, William said, "My guess is it will be the same people you hope are holding your hands when you die. A conversation about Wills can reframe the importance of developing deep, enduring relationships with friends, cousins, whoever, in the absence of immediate family. That you don't have children shouldn't lessen in any way your right to leave your money with someone or some organization to honor your life's work and your father's work. When you can answer the question, 'who are my emissaries?' I guarantee you'll begin living a purposeful life knowing you have started something extraordinary that can be continued. When you will with wisdom, it's wisdom that you will – this is your gift."

> When you will with wisdom it is wisdom you will...

With impeccable timing the waiter appeared with a basket of bread. "Your dinners will be out shortly." The lounge was getting busier and he seemed to vanish quicker than before.

Steve leaned toward Ashley. "You can still call me," he said, lightening the mood. "I do more than just write Wills. I also do family meeting facilitations. I have these great questions that I use. Though as it stands I only have three – I could use about four more."

"Yeah, yeah. I'll pick up the pace," William said. "I guarantee you'll have all seven questions before you finish your steak."

"Not so fast," said Steve. "Before you move on to the next question, I need something clarified. When you ask someone how an inheritance will advance their dreams for themselves, their family and their community and someone answers, 'I'll buy a car and a house,' doesn't that sound a little self-indulgent compared to giving money to buy lunches for hungry children?"

"I can only share my own family story," replied William. "Every family is different. In our family, everyone kind of answers in a similar way – we talk about how inherited wealth could be used to fund our own care when we are old, fund our children's education, pay down debt and help support our children as their lives unfold. There isn't a lot of talk about buying this or that. The real focus is on health and education, two priorities that have never taken a backseat to anything. I don't want to give the impression that we're monks – we live full lives, just not excessive ones."

"Hold it, William," interjected Steve. "It just occurred to me – what if someone says, 'I can't tell you what my dreams are until you tell me how much you're thinking of giving me.' What then? That's a legitimate question, isn't it?"

"Well, we have come to the most controversial part of our family's process. In our family there is transparency – always has been. At eighteen I asked my parents that very question: How much were they planning on leaving me? Do you know, my parents didn't hesitate for a second. In fact they went further and told me what their total assets were. It was a real conversation stopper. I remember thinking, wow, that's a lot of money. It was then that my parents mentioned their plans for retirement. They reminded me that both sides of our family live long lives – well into their eighties at least, and most into their nineties. I can still see my father taking out a pen and paper and scribbling some numbers that showed how much money they would need to live independently for thirty years after retirement with no income other than the return on their invested savings. He taught me about the corrosive effects of inflation, and all of a sudden that number didn't look so large. By giving that number a little context they taught me valuable lessons about money and time."

"I think these are the lessons most people hope their children will randomly trip over during their life," said Ashley.

"So you're saying everyone should tell their eighteen-year-old children what they're worth and what the kids will get? Because I have to say, this one's a deal breaker for me," said Steve.

"Absolutely not," replied William. "Whether someone shares this or not is a personal call. It depends on the maturity of the child and the strength of the relationship. If it's not there, then don't share."

"But without sharing, how will the maturity develop," asked Ashley. "What comes first, the chicken or the egg?"

"The quick answer is that everyone is different. The concept here is recognizing that you should share the contents of your Will before you die if you want to leave heirs who are prepared and who'll *grow*, not *decline*, as a result of your gift. But remember we don't know when we will die, so every year that we wait to prepare our children for their gift, the more we gamble with their future and the more likely that the gift will diminish their life."

Steve mumbled, "We gamble, that's for sure. It's just occurred to me that this whole process of talking about and writing a Will is about taking risks. Without taking risks there are diminished rewards. The easiest and least risky conversation is the one that's never had and that's why half the people who die have no Will."

"No question," replied William, "but here's the real lesson I learned the day I turned eighteen. I can still see my parents explaining that a Will isn't an old person's document. They said that unfortunate things happen all the time and people die unexpectedly." William paused, moved by his recollection of this story. "My parents said that if death were to come sooner rather than later for them, they wanted to make sure that my brother and I were prepared emotionally to receive our inheritance. It was a defining moment in our relationship. They said that as our parents, it was their duty and responsibility to teach us about money and ready us for that day, whenever it came. They said they didn't want us to be weighed down by our inheritance or beholden to it or mesmerized by it. They said that their friends told them they were crazy for sharing so much financial detail with their family and that it would wreck their kids, making us lazy and indifferent to working hard, knowing what was coming our way. My parents said they told their friends that children who are treated as adults, who are taught to respect money, not fear it, and who understand that wealth is earned by risking something of themselves, grow up to be productive citizens who master money by being neither controlled by nor in awe of it."

"You grew up in an interesting house," noted Steve.

"I did. Let me speak specifically about my father. He has the most amazing steely blue eyes, and I'll never forget that day partly because he stared into my eyes and taught me to grow up and understand that wealth is what we *make* it. He used an expression I've never forgotten: 'How we make it, is what we make it.' The day he shared his financial secrets, his personal net worth, is the day we both took a step forward. He a step closer to a good death knowing he was preparing me the way his father had prepared him, and me with a deep sense of obligation to honor the wisdom he shared with me that day. It's a wisdom I've shared with my own children. But," William paused, "wrapped around this financial openness was a clear warning to respect the *confidentially* of what had just been revealed. It was a moment marking the establishment of Family Inc., the business side of the family, and I had just been invited inside the tent. At eighteen, I was reminded that I was no longer a child and that my long journey of hard work and struggle was just beginning. The idea of retiring at eighteen was as likely in our family as winning the lottery. And just as winning the lottery is only an idea, the knowledge of an inheritance in our family is just that, *knowledge*; nothing less and nothing more."

Ashley shook her head. "I can't tell you how different your family treats the subject of money compared to mine. If I have this right, you're saying that if we plan to leave family with money and we are concerned about how it will affect their life, then we have the discussion now – don't wait, because people don't become masters of money the day a family member dies. It has to be taught and reinforced through discussion every day. Money and property are only a gift when they are given away – notionally given – when people are alive."

"Bingo," said William. "*Notionally given* is precisely it. When we release our grip on our possessions precisely when we acquire them, we stare death in the eyes and ready ourselves for it, whether it comes early or late. The shortage of drama in our family around money is the ultimate score card of my parents' success at raising financially fit children. The knowledge of what awaits my brother and me financially when my parents are dead is nothing more than wind in our sails today, helping us create our own wealth, in our own way, by taking risks. A notional inheritance can be a liberating and powerful force when trust is built one conversation at a time, starting at an early age when the potential and limitations of money are taught with equanimity."

William buttered a piece of bread before he continued. "It takes hard work to create and sustain a family. But when it's done well, there is nothing more satisfying than a family that clearly plays the consummate long game, each member sacrificing and investing in each other's unknown potential."

The waiter arrived with their bottle of wine, followed by the food runner with their meals. The waiter did the fresh ground pepper routine, bid them to enjoy and was gone.

"This looks good," remarked Steve. "I'm seriously hungry. Bon appétit."

"Wait, wait," Ashley said. "First a toast to William: Thank you for sharing!"

They raised their glasses and drank. "And thanks to you two," William returned, "for helping me clarify my thinking. The more we've gotten into this whole subject of Wills, the more I think there really might be a book in this. If advisors used it to help families talk about their Wills, and get them written and shared, it could do a lot of good. The subject is so big and complex you can see why people don't talk about it and why people believe it's easier to just remain silent and put your Will off for another year and another and another."

"Well," said Steve as he cut into his steak, "with 7,000 people dying every day in North America, a lot of lives are touched by death every day, and for some it will be absolute sadness and chaos. So yes, it could do a lot of good. Let's say, for argument's sake, that the average person who dies has ten close family and friends. That's 70,000 people a day who need to hear your message. Actually," he corrected himself, "that's 70,000 people who need to read your book *before* their loved one dies." Adopting a Southern accent, Steve concluded, "Git 'er done!!"

"Well, if I'm going to git 'er done," William said in the same voice, "I'm going to have to pick up the pace, so here's question #4." Ashley and Steve scrambled to put down their knives and forks and grab their pens.

"Alright," said William, "this one's a beauty. Steve, I think you're either going to kill yourself laughing at this or you'll think it's brilliant – honestly, it could go either way.

Question #4: In the context of planning for the division of your assets, does fair mean fair or does fair mean equal? Who are you planning on leaving your wealth to, and will you share a copy of your Will with me?

Without letting Steve respond, Ashley jumped in. "I think I can see exactly where this question is going. Let's say one child has provided the majority of care for an aging parent and then the parent dies and leaves their estate split equally between, say, two kids. You're asking whether equal is fair."

"The example you use is actually something I watched my parents live through," William said. "It was my mother and father who provided the care for my grandparents for a decade when they were unable to drive or to live independently. It was at our family meetings that I learned that my grandparents compensated my parents *at the time* for the time they spent and it was considerable, the time I mean. The compensation was modest but fair and simply acknowledged my grandparents' gratitude. When my grandparents died, they left their estate equally split between their children. They accomplished fairness and equality at the same time. They left both concepts intact. They did this in the open with total transparency and zero drama.

"I think this next point is critical," said William. "We assign special meaning to someone's last Will as if it reflects their deepest, truest and most authentic intentions. A Will is a permanent public and legal record of someone's intentions and for many it remains the only *recorded* word of someone's deepest sentiments. When the concept of equality appears to be tilted in favor of one family member over others, you can see that hurt and bad feelings will begin the day someone dies, and they will cut deep. Regret, anger and sadness are just some of what someone feels who has been treated any way but equally. In our family, the time for compensating someone who is doing more of the heavy lifting for the parents – providing personal care, say – is when that work is happening.

We assign special meaning to a person's last will

"When Wills are drafted in isolation and kept secret, family may assume that something other than equality is driving the giving decisions. If a Will is all about equality and fairness, the person writing the Will would surely be enthusiastic about telling everyone, so the logic goes. The tragedy is the cost to family relationships when people learn that their assumptions were false and that equality was indeed a touchstone principle. The person doing the dying simply hadn't accounted for the hurt and damage that silence caused when they were alive."

"I can see all that," said Steve, "but let me ask you a question. What if a parent provides help – call it a hand up, not a handout – to one child but not to another while the parents are alive? Surely in this situation you would argue that the Will should be adjusted so that the estate is equalized on death, so that the child who received the early gift ought to receive less when their parent has died?"

"I know this is going to sound contrarian, but in our view, absolutely not. What happens in our family is that when a gift is made to one person, it is made to everyone at the same time, whether others have the same need or not."

"That's… bizarre," remarked Steve.

"Here's why we do it. We know that time is money. We understand that it is nearly impossible for those who are responsible for settling an estate to arrive at a number that brings fairness and equality back into balance and meets everyone's expectations after a parent has died – especially if the executor is a family member."

"Just let me agree here," interrupted Steve, "that the whole estate equalization concept *is* a bit of a myth. Someone is always left feeling like they got the short end of the stick."

"Yes, and we believe that if one child receives a gift ahead of others, the inequity steals from the relationship between siblings from that day forward. This is a classic example of money driving a family apart, not bringing them together. We also know that the gift to one child, say a down payment for a home after a child is married, can create an economic incentive for other children, who might conclude, in the absence of a family conversation, that the only way to receive the same gift is to get married. Now remember my earlier comments about how incentives can create unintended consequences. The gift says to one child, 'my parents love my brother more because he is married. I'm not married and they didn't give me a gift. Only married siblings are valued in our family.' Or only buying a home is important; whatever. Whether this assumption is correct or not, this is what children deduce both consciously and subconsciously. Parental approval is a powerful force that seldom diminishes with time.

"The only caveat would be that if a child is under eighteen, money would be set aside and held in trust. The larger point is that my parents never gave secret gifts. I guess they know there's really no such thing as secrets in a family – eventually everything will be revealed, and the hurt will start."

"Wise indeed, but this is so out of step with conventional estate planning thinking," Steve confessed.

"Going back to the example," said William, "it may be that one child neither gets married nor buys a house. If parents give money only to the married one, it feels like a reward for getting married or buying a house. If they give a gift of money to both, the real gift is not the cash but the wisdom of the *concept of equality.* This can empower each child to make decisions that are authentic and true to themselves with the financial support they receive."

"This raises a whole bunch of other issues, though," exclaimed Steve, pointing at William with his fork. "What if parents can't afford to give all their children an equal amount of money at the same time?"

"It likely means the gift being contemplated for one child is too generous," replied William. "If they can't afford equal smaller gifts to all their children at the same time, they may not be able to afford to equalize their giving in the future."

"Your family really does take equality and fairness to a whole new level," remarked Ashley.

"As I've said, sibling rivalry in our family is an abandoned concept. We don't compete for family resources, not money, not love and not approval. We know fairness is an unassailable concept from start to finish. We create sibling teams whose economic interests are aligned, not competing. But more importantly my parents treat gifts they make when they are alive with the same care and attention they give to gifts that will be made when they're dead. Gifts release potential or destroy potential. *How* we give is as important as *what* we give and *when* we give it."

"What I will concede," said Steve, "is that anything short of equality in death leaves family relationships… challenged, shall we say. Often when a family member undeservedly receives a larger portion of the estate they are set up to receive scorn, hostility and rejection from other family members."

"No question," agreed William. "And families that allow that to happen are wired for self-destruction. This falls into the category of unintended consequences. Whether the favored beneficiary has actually asked for more or not is beside the point. The aggrieved family members may assume they did. It is not the dead who are held to account for their decisions but the living. If someone wants to leave a family that functions after they have died, they must will with wisdom in the *present*. Equality among heirs is no guarantee of family harmony, but it is almost always present in an extended family that thrives after a family member has died."

"I can tell you," said Steve, "that without question this is the number one issue that gets most jilted family members all fired up and suing each other. It happens most often when the guy in the ground unwittingly leaves different asset classes to different family members, thinking the value is the same."

"But what's wrong with that?" asked Ashley.

"Let's say," said Steve, refilling the wine glasses, "you have a mother who dies and in her Will leaves cash to one child and the other kid is left the family cottage. Mom thought this was fair because the cash and the cottage are worth the same. But the person who inherits the cottage gets a huge tax bill, the child with the cash, not so much. And then all hell breaks loose. And let's not even get into who gets to use the cottage in August! If Mom had sat down with a good advisor and said, 'I have these assets; how can I write my Will so that from an after-tax perspective my children are treated equally?' The assets gifted to each may have been different but the concept of equality would be preserved."

William joined in. "And fairness doesn't happen by accident. It requires planning. Wealth advisors and insurance professionals can quarterback the entire process, they can be a resource and participate in your family meeting, communicate and coordinate with other professionals, such as your accountant and lawyer, and implement what you – the client – wants to accomplish. But remember that all of this only takes place after the family has done their own work. Anything less will be the advisor's will, not the client's. A responsible professional advisor – lawyer, accountant, wealth or insurance advisor – does not shy away from encouraging a client to write their Will."

"How about insisting?" suggested Ashley.

"Yes, *insisting*. Now *that's* the advisor you and your family want. Get one or keep one who acknowledges the preeminent importance of writing a Will and keeping it up to date. If my dentist can remind me to make an appointment every six months, surely people in the estate-planning universe can do the same when it comes to updating my Will every year."

"Huh," grunted Steve as he chewed. "Now that you've embarrassed me into acknowledging that I don't send out reminder notices to my clients – something I promise to correct," he raised his hand in the Boy Scout salute, "let me ask you what happens when someone skips a generation – you know, leaves money to their grandchildren instead of their children. How do fair and equal figure into that situation? 'Cause I see this all the time," said Steve, returning to his meal.

"Great question," replied William. "Again, all I can do is relate what happens in our family. Notice the last part of question #4 asks *who we intend to share our wealth with and whether we would share a copy of our Will.* There's logic here. By sharing my Will with my parents, they can see where my estate will flow. My Will informs their Will and their Will informs mine. It's an intergenerational logic that drives the passing of wealth in an intelligent, transparent and orderly way. Remember, we don't presume that the old die first, which is why we share our Wills in both directions. You can see that this requires *and* builds trust."

"As much as I can see the value of this approach," Steve replied, "I just don't see this sharing of the Wills thing taking place in my practice. What I see is someone writing a Will, keeping it secret and leaving a significant amount of money to grandchildren without any context. On death, grandchildren, usually when they turn eighteen, receive all or a portion of their inheritance. You've heard of Trust-fund babies? Well, there are millions who become and remain completely disconnected from their family, estranged from their parents because of their newfound financial independence."

"That situation stems from the impoverished Wills I mentioned before that destroy families from the inside out by undermining parent-child relationships," said William. "Disturbing the natural flow of money by skipping generations can destroy family with more unintended consequences and all because another Will was drafted in silence without any discussion about what is truly fair." With that, William twirled his last few strands of linguine.

"But you do understand," said Steve, "that there are often tax incentives that encourage the gifting of wealth by skipping a generation."

"Don't get me started," responded William, tossing his napkin down. "The tax code wasn't written in consideration of family dynamics or family system theory. That particular web of rules is a public policy document designed to encourage certain behaviors. I can't remember reading anything in it that provides an incentive to avoid family disintegration."

"I think that would be expecting a bit much from our politicians, who seem to have no idea how so many of the laws of our land undermine the concept of family," concluded Steve.

"I know that when the tax tail wags the dog, family decisions about money and children will be made for the wrong reasons," said William. "Oh sure, someone will save tax all right, but many will also destroy their family relationships and their wealth in the process, and usually in that order. This obsession with putting tax at the center of estate plans drives me to distraction. You know the old saying: 'When you're a hammer everything looks like a nail.'"

"In fairness, there are many accountants who know the limitations of accounting."

"Yes," agreed Ashley, "and they'll be the ones handing out this book you're going to write, William."

"I'll keep that in mind," William laughed. "When accountants encourage clients to do their own work first, the tax plan can be designed to help the client and their family, who know where they are moving as individuals and together as an economic unit. The best part is that when accountants and wealth advisors bring intergenerational solutions to a family's wealth management, it's not uncommon for the entire family to become clients. The transparency in the family about money matters shows up in the relationship with advisors – relationships that are long and deep. If an advisor isn't offering values-based planning, good luck growing the practice because not even the offer of lower-cost services is going to entice a family to switch. An advisor who is blissfully ignorant of intergenerational issues is one who likely hasn't done their own Will and is likely to mangle the transfer of their own wealth, along with their clients'."

Taking a sip of her wine, Ashley said. "The world would surely devolve into chaos without accountants, but I have to say the ability of some to deal head-on with the concept of dying is equal to my ability to advise my clients about that adjusted cost base or basis thing my accountant keeps rattling on about."

"No question," said William. "That's why in a world of ever-increasing specialization the qualities we look for in an advisor are the ability to talk about their own limitations and their willingness to collaborate with other professionals. They know where their own expertise begins and ends and aren't afraid to share this with their clients. That's how trust is built – and that's another quality we look for in our entire advisory team.

"To turn the subject back to the issue of wealth skipping a generation," said William, "grandparents can no more succeed at being parents to their grandchildren than parents can succeed at being grandparents to their own children. When family members stray beyond their roles, family relations can buckle under the confusion."

"Interesting," said Steve. "I've seen lots of grandparents who figure they can correct whatever shortcomings they had when parenting their children by using money to shape the lives of their grandchildren. And you're right – it can add all sorts of complexity to family dynamics. So I guess it's not that someone shouldn't leave money or possessions to their grandchildren, but rather it needs to be proportioned so as not to undermine the parent-child relationship, right?"

William nodded. "Many times a person considering their Will looks at the lifestyles of their children and concludes that they don't need the money. They see the house, the cars, the jewelry, the vacations, etc., etc. and conclude that all is well. But in the absence of a full and open discussion about money and finances, Wills can underestimate the financial needs of the next generation. With people living longer and retirement being longer – and therefore vastly more expensive – it is almost inevitable that grandchildren who receive much larger inheritances from their grandparents than do their parents will be called on to fund their parents' retirement. This creates a cultural dynamic that has no historical reference point for the family, one that is both complex and, for most, deeply humiliating."

Steve fired off another question, sounding like he was in court. "Getting back to the actual question, what if someone in the family doesn't want to share their Will or the state of their finances?"

"Well," responded William, "again that speaks volumes about where the needle on the family's trust meter sits. I would conclude that the family has lots of work to do, lots of issues to resolve before they can get down to the business of transitioning surplus earnings in a way that honors the very best that family has to offer."

"So in a way," said Ashley, "you can use the process of discussing your Will as a barometer to measure the health of specific family relationships…"

"Yes, and…"

Steve interrupted. "Before you go any further, William, I need to clarify a couple things. You're saying that *proportionately* money shouldn't skip a generation, correct?"

Your Will is a barometer of specific family relationships

"Correct."

"But what if an intended beneficiary, an adult child, has ample wealth and neither needs nor wants their parents' money?"

"In that situation," replied William, "the issue is neither one of *need* nor *want* but one of *responsibility*. You need to understand that our family's questions augment the role of the patriarchs and matriarchs. When money skips a generation it steals from the responsibility of parents to parent their children. Because we know that families repeat what they have learned and experienced, we have to ask how grand-children will dispose of *their* wealth when the time comes. Will *they* skip a generation, perhaps even if their children need the help, because this has been their experience? A family, regardless of their wealth, must develop a culture that impos-es discipline on the disposition of their assets. Family dynam-ics improve when transparency, convention and tradition drive giving decisions. I believe money should flow to the next generation, who can release the wealth to their children in time. It will become wealth that has been gracefully and wisely relinquished – a gift that keeps on giving, a gift that cements parent-child relationships, not one that undermines and confuses."

"But," Steve declared, cornering the witness, "if the giv-ing decisions are pre-ordained, why the need to even ask the questions in the first place?" He slapped the table. "Why even have the meeting?"

"The *order* of leaving money to generations is predeter-mined – but the *proportion* we leave family, versus friends, ver-sus charities is what's at the center of our family discussions. That's what our family's seven questions really zero in on. We recognize that everyone's financial situation is constantly evolving; that's precisely why we have the conversation each year."

"I get it; very cool," said Ashley. "I know that had my fa-ther asked me these questions, I would have said 'for goodness sake you don't need to make me the sole beneficiary, there's more money than I can or even want to spend; let's leave some to charity. Which ones do you want to support, which ones do you want me to supervise when you're not here?'"

William waited a moment, then said, "You mean when he's *dead*. Try saying it, Ashley. Try calling death what it is. *Passing away, gone, entering into rest* are all words meant to soften, disguise and distract us from what death is. You're father isn't *gone*, he didn't *leave*, he is *dead*. I can tell from the way you speak of him, the stories you tell and the way you tell them, that he lives on in your mind and heart and still shapes your view of the world. He is dead, but his wisdom – although more could have been shared – is very much alive in you and will be until your own last breath."

Looking down, Ashley whispered, "My father is dead. His wisdom is now mine to give." Slowly looking up to meet William's eyes, she smiled softly as if to acknowledge the gift of William's directness.

After waiting a moment to acknowledge the awkwardness that can creep into any conversation when someone's vulnerability is laid bare, Steve sat up as if to begin a speech of his own. "Look, William, I'm having a hard time picturing someone holding a meeting and asking these questions, which you say are meant to address how they will split their assets between family, friends and charity. I mean, I get how it would help, but I just can't see people doing it. Are you saying that *all* your intended beneficiaries should be in the same room together – family, friends and charities?"

"Absolutely. In our family we use money to bring people together. Money can divide or money can connect, money can grow relationships or money can destroy them. Money is energy, it is there to employ."

"Hey, you're a poet, too!" laughed Steve.

William continued, "Money never waffles or equivocates. If you have it, the question is, do you control it, or does it control you? The answer lies in our engagement with others in our life. It's why some billionaires die impoverished, while some people of modest means who bask in the warm touch of family and friends die rich.

"But we're getting off track. I promised Steve I'd give him all seven questions before he finished his steak," Steve froze with his fork about to enter his mouth, "and either he needs to slow down or I need to speed up. Maybe we should just say you'll have all the questions before we finish dessert."

"Perfect," replied Steve.

"Okay, so let's keep moving. We could spend all night giving examples of the differences and similarities between *fair* and *equal* and debating how much to leave to the grandkids. Suffice it to say that the more a family talks the more likely it is they will arrive at a division of assets that is right for everyone. Ditto for friends and charities, although as you might expect, friends and charities, unlike family, are rarely absorbed and distracted by the concepts of fairness and equality. These are concepts that drive the *family* value system, rocket fuel that propels a *family* forward or makes it go ka-boom. So are you ready for question #5?"

Devouring his last piece of steak, Steve settled back into his chair and said, "Fire away, buddy." Again, Ashley and Steve grabbed their pens and readied themselves for the next salvo.

"My family's fifth question is, I think, the easiest," said William, "certainly the easiest for us because we've been at this a long time. But for someone just starting to talk with their beneficiaries, this question may be a bit more daunting. I'll explain the logic behind the question in a moment.

Question #5: Describe how your parents divided their assets and when you first learned of the contents of their Will. What would you do the same and what would you do differently?

"I'm getting the hang of these questions," said Ashley. "I think I see what this one is trying to accomplish. It's asking people to reach back into the past again to shape the future."

William nodded. "It's another question about retelling the family story. When we do this long enough, the stories become embedded as lore and the retelling becomes tradition.

But as you can see from the question even tradition must remain flexible to reflect newfound wisdom."

"I like that this process is flexible," replied Ashley. "It doesn't hold *perfection* as the goal but rather *continuous insight*."

"Indeed. For this question my parents' answers have always been pretty short and snappy. I'm paraphrasing but they usually say something like this: 'Our parents divided assets equally among siblings. Gender and birth order were irrelevant. There were provisions in the Will for a modest amount of money to go to grandchildren, to a family friend and to a handful of charities.'

"When asked what they would do the same as their parents, my parents say they would honor the family tradition and pass on as much cash as possible. My parents always explain that as my grandparents got older they sold more and more of their possessions with the idea that when they died the estate would hold just cash. Aside from a couple of sentimental items, my grandparents' Wills called on the executor to first distribute all liquid assets – cash, investments, that sort of thing. They instructed the executor to then arrange the sale of all other property, like the house and the car and so on. They made it clear that family always had the last look at any offer – in other words, the opportunity to top the highest offer that came from outside the family. The cash distributed to family and friends named in the Will exceeded the value of the remaining property, making it theoretically possible for one person in the family to purchase all the noncash assets. The proceeds from the sale of those assets were then distributed to the beneficiaries in the same proportion as the cash."

"That's an interesting approach," observed Steve. "I don't think I've seen an estate settled this way."

"But think about it," replied William. "My grandparents had named four beneficiaries, so after everyone had exercised their will and bought any items they wanted from the estate, everyone would receive a final check from the estate for a quarter of the value of property sold, including any items they themselves had purchased. In other words, anyone named in the Will who purchased any assets did so at a twenty-five percent discount. My grandparents called this their *Gift then Buy* estate plan. After this exercise was complete, the estate was settled and the file closed."

"It's brilliant," replied Ashley. "All the bickering, jealousy and petty fighting over *stuff* is replaced with a fair and transparent process that divides assets, not families."

"Fairness, equality, everyone doing what's right and best for themselves *and* their family. Principles of fair market value are honored and best of all, no fighting because my grandparents spoke with everyone about exactly how it would work for twenty-five years before they died. Here's the best part: Everyone's exercising control over their affairs. There's no willing from the grave, no one placing property in the hands of a beneficiary, saying, 'if you do this, I'll give you that.' I have no idea how long this has been going on in our family, but I'm certain that at the very least my great-great-grandparents willed with wisdom in this way."

"How did your parents answer the part about what they would do differently?" asked Ashley.

"They simply said that they would sell even more stuff than their parents did. They said they knew for sure that whatever value they placed on something, that value would diminish the farther it traveled through time away from the person whose labor and intellect earned the money to purchase it in the first place. Some believe that the longer something stays in the family the more it is valued. For others, when tough economic times come, the first piece of wisdom is that you can't feed your family sentimentality – and so shazaam, off to market goes the bear skin rug that great-great-great-grandpa Henry bought 150 years ago. And guess what? Although it had sentimental value, the fact that no one who ever met Henry is still alive makes it a little easier to redeem it for the more-needed cash."

"I can guess what gets sold last," said Steve. "It's the stuff packed either with wisdom, things like books, letters and journals, or packed with emotion, like jewelry and watches, things worn close to the body of the people who have died."

"Man, is your family efficient and practical or what?" exclaimed Ashley.

"Interesting choice of words," said William. "I would say that when it comes to death, dying and willing we aren't so much *practical* as we are *practiced*. We work hard on our own death, the past informing the future for the benefit of the unborn whom we will never meet. It is they who, despite sharing our DNA, are best described not as family, but as our future *humanity*."

"Am I correct in assuming that this question needs to be adapted slightly when being posed to a charity?" asked Steve.

"It does. Charities obviously don't have parents, but they do have founders. For charities my parents were considering including in their Wills, they worded the question this way: *Describe how the founders of your organization left their first gift to the organization. What would you ask new donors to do the same, and what would you ask them to do differently?*"

"That's a clever adaptation," remarked Ashley.

"Thanks. You can see that this is a question that can't be answered by someone unless they have a good grasp of their organization's history."

"Again, looking back before we look forward," said Steve, seeming pleased with his observation.

"The question is asking the charity to describe the mechanics of how the founders originally funded the organization and what they have learned is an effective way to leave money to the organization so that it can accomplish its current goals and objectives," explained William.

"And what sorts of things have you learned?" asked Ashley.

"First we learned how donors can harvest incredible information by asking a charity what it has done well and what it would change in terms of structured gifts. This question, more than any other, separates the wheat from the chafe. I have to say it is stunning how few representatives of charities know anything about the history of their organization, never mind how it was originally funded. Many have no clue what kind of bequests have worked well in the past and what kind of gifts have caused problems. Because we ask this question every year, we are really looking for an organization to demonstrate a capacity to learn. So if they fumble for an answer to the question the first time it's asked, it's really not the end of the world. It's really the following year that we take note – either they come back and give the same uninformed answer or they show us their capacity to grow and learn."

"These not-so-obvious questions," said Ashley, "are probing the kind of culture that exists in the charity. Is it a learning culture or is it one that's simply bureaucratic and indifferent to its own history? Does it have a clear picture of what its significant accomplishments have been and how it made them over the course of its history? Does it know its own shortcomings?"

"Precisely," responded William. "We want to know whether the values that lead us to earn and accumulate surplus wealth are alive in the organizations we are looking to support. We are looking for its people to be introspective but also inquisitive and entrepreneurial. For our family, it is those three qualities that our fifth question seeks to unearth. Others who use this question may be looking for a completely different set of values."

"Do you guys run a tight ship with your charitable giving or what!" said Ashley.

"We do. Remember the guy from the community foundation I mentioned earlier? When we asked him this question he told us that in 1954 the founders of the foundation had bequeathed a large sum of money to be used to provide assisted living for people who had polio. Well, obviously the advent of the polio vaccine meant that by the 1990s there was virtually no one left struggling with the disease. The restrictive nature of the gift meant that the board really couldn't honor the donor's original intent.

"The foundation rep told us the organization preferred to receive gifts that gave it flexibility to meet new and emerging needs. He talked about how needs change in a community but why it's nevertheless important for the organization to measure the impact that donated money makes and report back to the donor or surviving family. Gifts that give an organization *flexibility* but demand *accountability*, he explained, are the kinds of gifts that allow them to be creative, nimble and effective. Like I said, did this guy have our attention? You bet."

The waiter arrived to clear the remnants of their dinner and to ask whether they wanted to see the dessert menu.

Steve was first to respond. "Despite my earlier remarks about watching my weight, let me be clear that my diet starts tomorrow – bring it on!"

The waiter handed them the dessert cards and waited while they made their selections. "I'll have the sticky toffee pudding," said Steve. Ashley selected blueberry crumble.

"Just a little more coffee for me, thanks," said William. "Okay, we're heading into the home stretch – only two questions to go. Are you two ready for the next one?"

"I'm ready, and curious. I'm wondering if you save the question about providing care for a parent to the very end," said Steve.

Before William could answer, Ashley said, "Nope, it's the next question."

"Are you sure you're not a mind reader?" asked William.

Pointing at William's notepad, she laughed. "No, I'm just really good at reading upside down."

7

A Death Built with Care

*Close your eyes and take a deep breath. Now think…
As you lie waiting for death and have lost your capacity to
speak, will you have anything left to say?*

Glancing down at his notepad, William let out a long sigh. "You know what? I think this next question is the toughest. It's clearly the most emotional, for me anyway. It really drives conversation about a subject that has changed profoundly for families. Without knowing the future, it feels like even more change is on its way. With extraordinary advances in medicine, we just aren't dying the way we used to. It's not catastrophic events that kill the vast majority of people. Medical intervention after a major health crisis and a longer, slower, more protracted decline characterize the way so many now die. Like never before, family care, or at least family advocacy and oversight of the provision of care, is central to our extended life."

"I can see this question is going to be a real beauty," said Steve.

"Before I share my family's sixth question I want to make one point crystal clear. In as much as those in the family who are named beneficiaries are usually also the ones who provide care for the dying, the provision or promise of care is neither a given nor is it a precondition to receiving money. Money, or the prospect of receiving money, is just about the worst incentive for providing care, for obvious reasons. If there's any doubt about the relationship between care and money, *silence* has likely shaped that relationship."

"That being said," replied Steve, "it is remarkable how many people attempt to use their wealth to control the care they receive."

"Sometimes this is a conscious decision," agreed Ashley, "and now I see that at other times it is likely purely subconscious, informed by the dying person's own experience of a parent keeping their Will secret, revealing it only from the grave."

"The skills required to die are so different from those required to live," said William. "Dying is all about relinquishing control. For many people, living is all about exercising control and acquiring wealth. When and how these people transition from living to dying is anyone's guess. What I do know is that the answer is more fruitfully harvested by talking with those we trust and love. And that doesn't just happen by coincidence late in life after the majority of our time with family has been spent in silence. The best death is the one we see coming, the one we look at with curiosity. You can see why we're appalling at the art of dying. The end isn't going to be particularly satisfying for anyone if someone can't master this one difference. This is especially true when someone is required to make decisions

> The best death is the one that we see coming

about, say, resuscitating you or not and there's no Will, no living will, no advanced directives, nothing but a history of silence. No real tangible measure of the love and trust in the relationship."

The waiter placed Steve's and Ashley's desserts on the table and refilled William's coffee cup. "Thanks," William said. As the waiter retreated, William continued. "You probably realize now that if a family has been using these questions for a number of years the person doing the willing has garnered a pretty good feel for who *loves* them or not. And isn't that what a Will is – a declaration of our love and hope for others to continue our work using our wisdom and wealth? As beneficiaries, either this sentiment is in us or it's not. It cannot be manufactured or feigned. And here is the hard part: There is a point, for most people, in the dying process when we lose our capacity to make decisions in our own best interests and must rely on someone to advocate for us. Who? Family usually. What kind of family? The family who has talked about your death repeatedly, who helped you write your Will, whose Wills you have shared? Or the one you've kept in the dark about all matters related to your life, money, dying and death because mistrust and fear defined your view of your family and the world? The ones who love you and know your wishes are the only ones who can advocate for the death you desire, not a doctor you've never met. Not to deride the medical profession but heads up – they don't love you, at least not the way your family can. They have a job to do and behind you are more sick people heading to their exit, people who are perhaps younger, healthier, and who the doctor may feel are perhaps more deserving of the doctor's finite time and other scarce resources. If you don't think you'll need someone advocating for your life you don't understand dying in the modern world."

"That's put me off my pudding," moped Steve.

Ashley ignored him. "I've been there, been in that exact position. In effect, the gift you can give your family is the gift to speak and act on your behalf to say now is not the time, we need to try this medical intervention or that, or now *is* the time to say goodbye."

"In our family, the day we say goodbye feels familiar because it is," replied William. "It's the day we've spoken about so often, year after year, there's simply nothing left to say except, 'I promise to honor your wisdom. I will always love you. Goodbye.' This gift, whether you call it Power of Attorney for Personal Care, a Living Will or Advanced Healthcare Directives, is truly the ultimate gift. It's someone putting their life *and* their death in your hands."

"That families don't speak about this is nothing short of incredible," said Steve.

"It is," agreed William. "End-of-life decisions born from silence and uncertainty are worn like an anvil of shame and regret around survivors' necks, haunting them. How we execute our duties informs our own death, be that tomorrow or far in the future, when we hand over control to those we love – the ones we invited to play the lead role in our death.

"When it comes to care, no currency but love matters. Whether this care comes late in life or earlier than someone ever imagined, after an accident or an unexpected diagnosis, love, not money, is what inspires others to give their time and wisdom to protect your interests, to speak when you cannot and to help you die the way you described when you were thinking clearly. People must not wait for someone to be hooked up to life-support machines to begin the conversation about dying. In our family, we examine that mental image long before it becomes real and have that conversation today because we know that that day may in fact come sooner than expected."

After pausing to sip his coffee, William continued. "It is a choice to die while relinquishing control to others. This is how we *unlearn* our fear of death, simply through our trust in love and our love in trust. Love and trust. There can be no better way to die than with both our hands being held – one hand informed by the past and the other informing the future.

"You'll see that this question, like the previous ones, leaves room for personal growth and for new wisdom to emerge. Our questions acknowledge that we never stop learning, right up to the moment we die. The potential to learn what we can't know on our own can only be fulfilled through our interdependence with those we love."

"Our family's sixth question is based on that concept – it's another one that asks us to look to the past to inform the future.

Question #6: Describe the role you play or played in the final care of your parents. Can you name one thing that was or is being done well, and one thing you could change or wish you had done differently?

"When my mother raises this question in our family meetings, she almost always answers it first before anyone else can respond. She is so eager to go over the fifteen years she spent providing care for her parents. When describing what she had done well, she speaks of the integrity she tried to bring to the process. She tells about keeping her parents in their home as long as possible, weighing the benefits of doing so against the risks to their health and safety, and the same when it came to their driving – and then not driving when the last accident almost proved fatal. The balance she struck between preserving both their dignity and their safety was methodical and to a certain extent heart-wrenching. Curtailing the freedom of parents who gave us our freedom is not easy. There's no sugarcoating just how difficult it was to walk this balance every day. When she describes how her parents' decision to stop driving meant that she began her new career as a taxi driver, shuttling them to appointments and social functions, we can see the pride and satisfaction in her memories. It was hard but familiar work that took her back to when she did the same for her kids. She talks about how odd it was to be parenting her children and her parents at the same time. Everything old is new again, she says as she recounts those fifteen years."

"Fifteen years is a long time to provide care," said Ashley. "I had three tough years with my father – fifteen seems unimaginable."

"And let me tell you it was bizarre watching my parents, whom I saw as elderly, taking care of my ancient grandparents," said William. "Advances in medicine are changing everything and it's only going to get more interesting as our love affair with technology supplants our good judgment to say 'enough is enough; my work here is done.'"

"What about the last part of the question," asked Ashley, "the part about what could have been done differently with regard to providing care? How did your folks answer that?"

"You can see my mother's confusion and equivocation year in and year out when she acknowledges her efforts to keep her mother alive as long as she did," said William. "She has described how her love clouded her judgment to the extent that, paradoxically, she prolonged her mother's life beyond what was probably best. Despite a family culture of talking and sharing perspectives on death, not enough detail, she explained, had been shared with respect to *advanced directives*. My mother wears her doubts on her sleeve every day. It's an extraordinary thing, she says, to be given the power to provide peace for your parents and then not exercise it because of your own fear of death."

"I feel your mother's uneasiness," affirmed Ashley. "Unless you go through it, it's hard to imagine holding a parent's life in your hands."

"Indeed," continued William. "By sharing this story she is saying, 'for goodness sake, please don't make the same mistake with me! Here is what death looks like for me; if you see and hear what I'm describing, please don't resuscitate. Please give me this gift and know that you have honored my hard-earned wisdom.' And by *see and hear* she means see and hear from medical professionals words like *irreversible decline, no brain activity* and *irreversible vegetative state*. She has been precise and exacting, looking at her own death through the lens of her mother's death and knowing exactly how she wants it to be. She knows she may need our help in death and asks if we were willing to receive her wisdom and deliver her gift."

"Dissipating the fear of death, giving and taking – reciprocating Wills, evolving Wills – this is a practical example of what you've been describing all evening," said Ashley.

"When my father answers this question he has sometimes remarked on how well he worked with his brothers and sisters to arrive at a caring plan that provided dignity for both his parents as they neared their deaths. He talked about how he handled the finances while his sister, who lived closer to their parents, provided the care. There was a division of labor – not equal in terms of time and effort – but a contribution from everyone in the family. Using money from the estate to compensate those doing more of the heavy lifting was a plan hatched by sharing thoughts at their family meetings decades before anyone required assistance. Sibling rivalry just didn't come up, and that's a dividend earned as he approaches his own death.

"To the question of what he would have changed with respect to the care his parents received, his answer is personal and touching. He has described how his mother was an avid reader, and he wished that as she neared death and lost her sight he could have read to her at her bedside more often, the way she had done when he was a child. Now if you're wondering if I'll be reading to my father if he can't read as he nears his death, then you're getting the hang of how these questions and our family work. Sharing our regrets and our vulnerabilities is how we release the potential for something better for *ourselves* when we teach our children how to listen and learn from our own misgivings."

William paused to let Steve and Ashley absorb and reflect on what they were hearing.

"Now of course," he continued, "this question is also asked of charities, and what we have learned is remarkable. The charity that was so dear to my grandparents' hearts was incredibly supportive in the last stage of their lives. To be specific, my grandfather received lovely caring visits from the volunteers of that organization and money was never discussed. The meaningful relationship between charity and donor was both deep and longstanding.

"There's so much more I could share about our family's response to this question, but let me just conclude that individuals who have no children can and should use these questions to begin a dialog with friends. Increasingly, it's friends who are being invited to participate as executors and empowered to provide end-of-life care. All the possibilities for a death well-planned are within reach when we can converse with friends as if they are family. In everything I've shared with you, you can substitute the word *friend* for *family*. Friendships cultivated over time can be enriched today when we invite people to talk about our death and about their death, in the same reciprocating and evolving way."

"I'm seeing this more often," agreed Steve. "With the move to smaller families fifty years ago, and with families spread out across the country and around the globe, I'm seeing friends stepping in and playing these roles as executors and with powers of attorney."

"I know there was a time this evening, Steve, when you thought you weren't going to get any of my family's seven questions," William said with a smile. "But we've really zipped along here. And I hope that shows how quickly a family can use these questions to build their own discussion. So drum roll, please: Here is my family's seventh and final question. It's not going to surprise you that we conclude our family meetings on our birthdays with a question that's like closing our eyes and making one last wish before we blow out the candles.

Question #7: Describe in detail your last wishes.

"Blow out the candles – nice!" laughed Ashley.

"When we use the term *last wishes* we are really talking about final arrangements – how our life will be celebrated and our body relinquished. For many people, religious beliefs and customs prescribe in great detail how it will be. But in an increasingly secular world and even for those with religious traditions, the options for one's celebration of life, funeral, memorial service, whatever you want to call it, are changing faster than the manager of your local bank. And you couldn't pick a worse event to plan under the pressure of time, with every grieving family member weighing in on the subject, only to find that everyone has a different and inflexible vision. And without a family discussion well in advance, that's what you're going to get."

"I hear about this from my clients all the time," said Ashley. "It's a huge and confusing challenge for surviving family and friends to make these decisions when they are grieving – especially when money is an issue."

"I once spoke at a funeral directors association conference – great bunch of people, by the way, very alive, very interesting; not at all what you'd imagine. Here's a story I heard from one of them. Mom dies and the three daughters each have their own rendition of where they remember their mother expressing a desire for her remains to be placed. One daughter recalled her mother wanting to be buried alongside her own parents hundreds of miles away from where she lived, another daughter remembered the mother wanting to be cremated and interred in the same local cemetery as their father, and the third daughter – the youngest – was emphatic that her mother had expressed a desire to be cremated and her ashes spread equally on the east coast and the west coast because she had lived on both. Whether these recollections were accurate or reflected what each daughter wanted for herself is beside the point."

"Oh my," responded Ashley, shaking her head. "What happened?"

"The mother had designated in her Will that the youngest daughter would be the only executor of the estate given that she lived the closest. What most people don't realize is that the executor has the power to make decisions about final arrangements – there doesn't need to be a vote. Democracy doesn't hold sway in estate planning unless of course equality and fairness are reflected in the Will."

"And…" prompted Ashley, waiting for the outcome of the story.

"It seems the youngest daughter was all about efficiency and not about forging a consensus. Despite warnings from her sisters that they would never speak to her again if she divided their mother's ashes across the country, she forged ahead. Not only that, but the funeral was extremely long and formal, reflecting the youngest daughter's more orthodox religious beliefs. The mother, in fact, hadn't been religious at all. The decision to have an open casket was the tipping point for one of the daughters, who simply refused to attend the funeral. What do you think the grandchildren of that dead woman will take away from this death?"

"That death is chaotic…" replied Ashley.

"Yep," replied Steve.

"…that death pulls families apart…" said Ashley.

"Unfortunately yes," replied William.

"…and that we mustn't speak about death and that the future is destined to repeat the past," concluded Ashley.

"Bingo," said William. "No Wills, no talk of Wills and definitely no talk about *last wishes*, which should be all about the celebration of life. Silence around these matters ensures that the family won't be coming together to soak up wisdom and reflect on a life that has ended. The opportunity of death is squandered and replaced with anger, jealousy, competition and most of all, regret. The legacy left is the destruction of a family."

"Devastating," said Ashley.

"Now do we really believe this was the final wish of this mother? This acrimony had nothing to do with money and everything to do with power and control, the very thing she failed to exercise when she was healthy and thinking clearly. Her death wasn't a gift, it was the opposite of a gift. What's the word I'm looking for?" asked William.

"A liability?" answered Steve.

"Yes! She may have died with surplus wealth, but she left her family a liability, an emotional debt that steals from everyone."

"What an epic failure at death and dying," Ashley commented.

"And," added William, "failure at living. I think talking about final arrangements is the icing on the cake, not for the dead but for those left behind who need to say goodbye together *and* alone. The final arrangements aren't so much a closure as they are a transition to a new relationship with our loved one, who is dead but whose wisdom is very much alive. Final arrangements can be an inspiring gift that we leave for family, friends and community or they can be nothing but thoughtless indifference, just the way life itself was approached and lived."

After a few moments of silence, Steve spoke up. "I'm pretty sure most people think of a Will as just a legal document that divides assets – full stop. But for me, the penny has dropped this evening: After talking about death, our relationships with our family, friends and community can fully mature, and our life can become purposeful in the service of others. Our fear of death recedes."

"That's an excellent summary," replied William. "Let me finish by offering a little perspective. We have spent the entire evening talking about dying and death. You might get the impression that my family is a bit obsessed with death. But you need to remember that our family conversations about Wills and dying only take place on our birthdays, and often for less than an hour. Once it's done, it's done. Ashley, you spoke of living a purposeful life; well, that's what we really do on each of our birthdays and every other day of the year. And we can do so because the way has been cleared. We're *not* a death-obsessed family – quite the opposite. In fact, I can't remember ever talking about Wills and dying anytime except at family meetings on birthdays."

"Well, I really think you *should* write a book," said Steve. "You need to spread this message. And I have to say before we shut this party down: William, you have opened my eyes to greater possibilities in my profession."

"I am humbled."

After pausing, looking down and clearly struggling for words, Steve continued. "I have a confession to make and it's not easy – it's not something I'm proud of. I haven't exactly been fully forthcoming this evening."

William and Ashley waited.

"I... I haven't updated my Will in over fifteen years. And I certainly haven't spoken to my kids about what's in it," stammered Steve. "For Pete's sake, I'm like the shoemaker with barefoot children. So here's my commitment to myself and to you two. From this day forward, the way I'm going to practice estate law is going to change. I'm not going to draft clients' Wills, I'm going to help them discover their own wisdom and to share it with the people they love. But only after I've done my own work, after I've held my own family meeting and used these seven questions. And then I'm going to send a letter to every single one of my clients."

"This is awesome," William said. "What's the letter going to say?"

"Short and sweet, really. Something like,

> 'Dear Client,
> With your birthday fast approaching, let me extend my best wishes.
>
> I'm writing to remind you that it's been a number of years since you last updated your Will. A Will is the most important legal document in your estate plan and it is my professional responsibility to help you keep yours current.
>
> The consequences of not updating your Will reach far beyond the financial and will affect your family today and after you die.
>
> I would like to meet with you and share seven questions that will help you and your beneficiaries shape your Will.
>
> I will call you shortly to make an appointment.
> Sincerely,' etc., etc."

"That's fantastic!" said Ashley. But then she looked down, studying the table briefly before looking up again. "And since we're making confessions, I have one of my own. Before I do, though, Steve, let me say that as an estate lawyer, what you just told us couldn't have been easy to say out loud, so thank you. And now to reciprocate. As embarrassing as it is to say, I have no Will *at all*. My father's death and the chaos that followed winding up his estate made my Will just about the last thing I wanted to consider – until tonight. I can see now that I have the wisdom to set a new standard for my family, friends and community. So thank you both for sharing your insights."

"I've also learned a valuable lesson tonight," said William. "I had assumed that both of you had Wills and that they were up to date. It's something I do too frequently – make assumptions, that is. If I do write this book to help families find their will to will, I need to do a better job of asking questions beyond the seven I've shared tonight. On a positive note, I'm thrilled that you two are going to get cracking on your Wills in collaboration with the people and organizations important to you – that's two down, 124 million and change to go!"

Laughing, Steve replied, "What do you say we change the subject and talk about something completely unrelated to Wills and death and dying?"

"Good plan," agreed Ashley.

Steve said, "I heard that Cirque du Soleil has a new show over at the Bellagio. Apparently two performers do a death-defying high-wire act with never-before-seen stunts. Are you two game for the late performance?"

"Absolutely," said William. "And I'll bet you ten bucks one of those aerialists doesn't have a Will!"

The Will to Will Campaign

125 million United States and Canadian citizens over the age of 18 have no legal Will. The Will to Will Campaign is dedicated to raising awareness about the importance of discussing, drafting, signing and sharing your Will with beneficiaries.

How can you help? You can start by sharing your own story. Comments can be left anonymously – no email address or personal information is required. Visit

www.WillingWisdom.com

and click on Readers' Comments.

Only through sharing real-life stories can others learn why it's important to have a lawyer prepare their Will and keep it up to date. We all have something valuable and positive to leave to the ones who matter most in our lives – even if what we leave isn't money.

Further Reading

Ernest Becker. *The Denial of Death*. Simon & Schuster, 1973.

Stephen R. Covey. *The 7 Habits of Highly Effective Families*. Golden Books, 1997.

Stephen Jenkinson. *Money and the Soul's Desires: A Meditation*. Stoddart, 2002.

Anthony de Mello. *Awareness: The Perils and Opportunities of Reality*. Doubleday, 1990.

Adam Phillips and Barbara Taylor. *On Kindness*. Farrar, Straus & Giroux, 2009.

Irvin D. Yalom. *Staring at the Sun: Overcoming the Terror of Death*. Wiley, 2008.

Irvin D. Yalom. *The Yalom Reader: Selections from the Work of a Master Therapist and Storyteller*. BasicBooks, 1998.

Public Speaking

The *Willing Wisdom* Keynote Speech is for

- Top-tier investment and insurance professionals dedicated to helping their clients with their estate planning
- Legal and accounting firms dedicated to successful client wealth transfers
- Employers wanting to educate employees about estate and retirement planning
- Industry associations dedicated to preparing their members' succession plans
- Philanthropic organizations committed to educating donors and prospective donors about planned giving
- Family offices

For speaking fees and availability please contact Détente Financial Press Ltd. at
sales@WillingWisdom.com
or by phone at 519-940-4655.

Dr. Deans is a frequent speaker in New York, Chicago, San Diego, San Francisco, Las Vegas, Phoenix, Dallas, Miami, Toronto, Calgary and Vancouver. Discounts on travel are available for back-to-back bookings.